EASTERN COACH WORKS
1946-1965

Front Cover Illustration

Amongst the ranks of preserved ECW vehicles the Bristol KSW6B owned by Robin Woodcock and
Adrian Hunt is a prime example of the standard product. Typical of highbridge KSWs throughout the
country and absolutely representative of the Bristol fleet it first entered service on New Year's Day
1956 with Bristol Tramways & Carriage Co. After some 17 years service it passed straight into
preservation, during which time it spent eleven years in the open. It passed to its present owners in
September 1992. It may be hard to believe that despite those eleven years it has not been repainted
since 1982. The destination shown is that used for a return workers service which followed an
afternoon school trip. Described as a very sound vehicle indeed, with four speed gearbox and Bristol
AVW engine, it will return 15 mpg when driven carefully. Peter Durham produced the excellent
photograph and looks forward to producing more work for Venture.

Typeset and produced electronically for the Publishers by
Mopok Graphics, 128, Pikes Lane, Glossop, Derbyshire
Printed and bound in Great Britain

EASTERN COACH WORKS
1946 – 1965

by
Maurice Doggett
and
Alan Townsin

Principal Photographers in this Volume

Geoff Atkins
Maurice Doggett
Roy Marshall

VENTURE PUBLICATIONS LIMITED   PO BOX 17 GLOSSOP DERBYSHIRE

CONTENTS

Westcliff's lowbridge K5G AJN 825, new in 1939, carries the oldest unmodified ECW body, and is seen regularly at rallies.

Southern National ETT 956, a 1938 L5G new to Western National, lengthened in 1955, was rebodied. It is seen at Torside, Derbyshire returning from a rally.

Thames Valley DBL 154, a 1946 built standard lowbridge K6A.

Wilts & Dorset NAM 116, a 1955 built LS5G seen in service in Salisbury in 1968.

All photographs J. A. Senior.

CONTENTS

Bristol Omnibus 1960 built MW5G type 994 EHY seen in service in 1969.

Crosville SC4LK type 904 OFM built in 1960, carrying 35-seat 'coach' body seen at a rally.

Red & White RESL type LAX 107E built in 1967 in service in Cardiff in 1968. (See next volume for full details of this type).

Eastern Counties 5615 NG, a 1961 built FS5G Lodekka with enclosed platform, seen in service in Norwich in 1969.

All photographs J. A. Senior

Venture Publications Ltd
– a new name in transport publishing

Founded in May 1993 by a group of transport professionals including authors, researchers, historians, editors, publishers, photographers, operators and businessmen, Venture Publications Ltd will serve the needs of the discerning transport enthusiasts, as well as providing material to which the student may turn in his or her research into the history of road transport. Its output will be concentrated mainly on the bus and truck and light rail/tramway scene, but heavy rail subjects will also feature. Quality and accuracy will be its twin aims at all times.

Venture is fortunate in being able to call on the talents of many well-known people in the transport publishing business. Alan Townsin, one-time editor of *Buses Illustrated* and later for many years with Transport Publishing Company, will be Editor-in-Chief. John Senior, with a lifelong career in print and publishing, will handle design and production, whilst Mark Senior will act as Venture's sales agent. A mail order service will be operated through PO Box 17 Glossop SK13 9FA, and customers will be welcome by prior appointment once the office, shop and warehousing facilities have been established. Trade distribution will ensure Venture's books will be available in leading transport bookshops.

Writers will include Alan Townsin, T. B. Maund, Doug Jack, Neil MacDonald, Maurice Doggett, Colin Morris, Richard Hills, Stanley King, John Carroll, Scott Hellewell, Eric Ogden, Harold Nancollis, Stuart Broatch and many other specialists whose names are already a byword in transport publishing.

Venture's first titles will include a two-part history of Ribble Motor Services by T. B. Maund; Eastern Coach Works 1946-1965 and, subsequently, 1965 to closure by Maurice Doggett and Alan Townsin; Leyland – the Workington Bus Factory story by Doug Jack; a two-part history of Southdown; Bradford's Trolleybus history; other major manufacturer's histories including Blue Triangle, a revised version of the history of AEC buses, by Alan Townsin; Bedford and Foden.

Other titles in the pipeline will be announced in *Classic Bus*, *Buses*, and other enthusiast's magazines, and also in Venture's regular mailing shots. To ensure you receive your copy send a sae to Venture at the address below.

VENTURE PUBLICATIONS LIMITED **PO BOX 17 GLOSSOP SK13 9FA**

INTRODUCTION

It was hardly surprising that standardisation was a key aim at Eastern Coach Works Ltd, particularly in the period from 1946. Quite apart from the urgent need for new buses after nearly six years of war, Sir Frederick Heaton was Chairman of the Tilling group (to which about half the major bus operating companies in England and Wales belonged) and of ECW itself, and he believed in uniformity of practice and centralised control of many policy matters.

Yet in practice, there was variety too, to an extent which may come as a surprise to some readers, partly because of such factors as the rebodying of sound older chassis for many operators, and partly because of new technology. Both ECW and Bristol, as the bus chassis maker within the Tilling group, with which there was close association, were leaders of fresh thought in bus design.

An important factor affecting the story was the voluntary sale of the Tilling group's bus interests in 1948 to the newly-formed British Transport Commission, set up to control the nationalised transport industry that was a major aim of the Labour Government of the time. This tended to isolate the member companies, not least Bristol and ECW as manufacturers, from the rest of the industry. Under the rules laid down by Parliament, sales of ECW bodywork, or Bristol chassis, to operators outside the BTC were not allowed, once outstanding orders were fulfilled.

Yet those who think that public ownership and an absence of direct competition necessarily stultifies initiative should consider the Lodekka double-decker and the RE single-decker, both products of close co-operation between Bristol and ECW during their completely State-owned era. They were influential landmarks in the history of bus design as well as being reliable and efficient products capable of long trouble-free service.

During the period covered by this volume, ECW was strongly influenced by its three successive General Managers. William (Bill) Bramham had been appointed to the newly-formed company in 1936. When he left for pastures new in 1948, he was succeeded by J. W. (Bill) Shirley, who had been Works Manager since 1938. He in turn moved on in 1953 and R. E. (Ralph) Sugden began his long period of managership, continuing until 1970, when he died in office.

Bramham and Sugden both came to ECW from Charles H. Roe, the Leeds bodybuilding concern, and the Roe influence was not hard to find, especially in double-deckers, in ECW's early days. The post-war designs, so 'fresh' in character, surprisingly enough had their roots in a very liberal interpretation of the wartime 'utility' specification. Bill Shirley had been with Metro-Cammell in the early days of metal-framed bodies, so it was not surprising that ECW's switch to metal framing on a regular production basis roughly coincided with his appointment as General Manager. Ralph Sugden's background was more on the costing side – he had become Commercial Manager before becoming Deputy General Manager – but when putting this book together, it struck me that the production Lodekka LD-type, effectively the first product of the Sugden era, represented a distinct reversion to curvaceous outlines, rather in the Roe-influenced tradition, after a period when rather more upright styles had been in favour.

This book is based on Maurice Doggett's immensely detailed study of the company, which goes back for many years, with numerous visits to Lowestoft, and also his and John Senior's discussions with senior management. I, too, have memories of admiring most of ECW's new products as they first appeared, over the whole span of this volume. Yet working with Maurice's material has been a fascinating and immensely enjoyable task, revealing many facts of which I was unaware despite my own considerable interest in the firm. I hope that readers will find the result similarly engrossing.

This volume takes the story as far as 1965, not only about half-way to the end of production in 1987 but a year in which a major change of direction took place, with the beginning of ECW's association with the Leyland empire. The story of that, with its new opportunities but growing problems, will be told with a similarly detailed and illustrated story of the various types built in the next and final volume already in course of preparation. It will also include more on the people and the factory premises, as well as a review of ECW's influence on other concerns, with illustrations of many of the 'lookalikes'.

Alan Townsin
Steventon
1993

Thanks are due to all those who made photographs available for this volume. Apart from those identified individually below, Eastern Coach Works official photographs are used. Up to the end of 1959 they were taken by the local firm of Boughton & Sons of Lowestoft and the negatives of these have since been purchased by Mr S. J. Butler. From 1960 to the end of 1976, the photographic work for ECW was undertaken by Laurence Gall, also of Lowestoft, and in this case the negatives passed to Mr Brian Ollington of Gorleston who became the official ECW photographer from 1977, when he took over the Gall business. The co-operation of these gentlemen is acknowledged with thanks. Over the years many prints of these photographs were issued by ECW, and later Leyland, for publicity purposes, some of which are held on a personal basis by the author and editor. Others form part of collections which have been passed to Senior Transport Archives, and examples of all these have been used in preparing this book.

AEC/BCVM   11 (lower), 36 (centre), 73 (top)

G. F. Ashwell   62 (centre)

J. H. Aston   58

G. H. F. Atkins   12 (both), 13 (lower), 14 (upper), 16 (lower), 29 (bottom), 30 (top), 32 (top), 35 (top), 37 (top), 38 (top), 41, 44 (top), 47 (bottom), 48 (top), 56 (bottom), 61 (bottom), 63 (bottom), 75 (bottom), 77 (top & centre), 81 (bottom), 87 (centre & bottom), 96 (centre), 99, 100 (top), 101 (bottom), 102 (both), 105 (bottom), 108 (top), 129 (bottom), 133 (top).

Gavin Booth   66 (top)

BCV/BCVM   68 (bottom), 80 (top), 109 (top)

J. S. Cockshott   46 (centre)

A. B. Cross   42 (top)

M. G. Doggett   31 (top), 34 (top), 47 (top), 57 (centre & bottom), 59 (bottom), 62 (bottom), 70 (both), 71 (bottom), 73 (centre), 79 (bottom), 84 (top & bottom), 85 (bottom), 86 (top left), 88 (top), 89 (top), 93 (centre), 96 (bottom), 103 (top & centre), 105 (centre), 106 (both), 110 (top), 113 (bottom), 114 (bottom), 115 (all), 116 (all), 118 (centre right), 119 (top & bottom), 122 (bottom), 125 (bottom), 127 (centre), 128 (both), 131 (both), 132 (top), 133 (bottom).

M. G. Doggett collection   18 (lower), 31 (centre), 32 (bottom), 33 (bottom), 43 (bottom), 44 (bottom), 45 (all), 46 (bottom), 49 (bottom), 57 (top), 61 (top), 71 (top), 72 (centre), 73 (bottom), 76 (bottom), 78 (top & centre), 82 (centre & bottom), 85 (top & side), 86 (centre & bottom), 88 (bottom), 92 (bottom), 95 (top), 96 (top), 100 (bottom), 114 (top), 119 (centre), 120 (top), 121, 123 (top), 126 (lower).

A. J. Douglas   92 (centre)

Peter Durham   Cover

Eastern Daily Press   104 (top)

E. D. Hodgkins   40 (bottom)

A. E. Jones   30 (bottom), 46 (top)

T. W. W. Knowles   134 (top)

R. F. Mack   92 (top)

P. J. Marshall   72 (top), 79 (centre)

R. Marshall   9, 30 (centre), 34 (bottom), 36 (top), 49 (centre), 52 (bottom), 55 (bottom), 72 (bottom), 77 (centre), 86 (top right), 87 (top), 89 (bottom), 93 (centre), 95 (bottom), 98 (bottom), 100 (centre), 101 (top), 110 (bottom), 113 (top), 117 (bottom)

G. Mead   35 (lower), 60 (bottom), 67 (top), 83 (top), 94 (top), 95 (centre), 114 (centre), 117 (centre), 120 (centre), 126 (top), 132 (bottom)

J. Pettie   66 (bottom two)

M. Mogridge/P. Sposito   80

Real Photographs Ltd   83 (bottom)

P. J. Relf   61 (centre)

J. A. Senior   Colour material for contents

Senior Transport Archives   62 (top), 82 (top)

Senior Transport Archives/R. N. Hannay collection   60 (top), 77 (bottom), 111 (centre)

R. H. G. Simpson   43 (top), 74 (top)

D. M. Stuttard   117 (top)

Surfleet Transport Photos   67 (lower)

A. A. Townsin collection   10 (upper), 13 (upper), 52 (centre), 65 (all), 94 (bottom), 97 (top), 105 (top)

M. J. Tozer   75 (top)

Vectis Transport Publications   51 (top)

A. M. Wright   36 (bottom)

The LS-'Light Saloon' was typical of mid-'50s ECW single-deck production. The 45-seat ruggedly constructed vehicle incorporating Bristol-built underframe weighed just over 6 tons – comparable with today's midibuses. Western National 1767, delivered in 1955, like most was a Gardner five-cylinder example.

ACKNOWLEDGEMENTS

I first became aware of the products of ECW in 1946, when living in a house alongside the A11 road at Barton Mills, West Suffolk, for Bristol chassis would pass bound for Lowestoft and gleaming complete new buses would return in the opposite direction. My first visit to the premises was on an Omnibus Society visit in 1957, my group being shown round by Mr Ted Godley, who had worked there since the Eastern Counties days. Contact with him continued for some time and it is he I have to thank for my initial insight into the workings of the factory, as well as supplying copies of the weekly production sheets. When he died, my new contact was Mr Ernie Besford, though I had also met Mr Jack Lewis of the drawing office and who allowed me access to information on pre-war production.

During the last ten years of ECW's existence, I met and talked to many other members of the staff, the introductions being through John Senior, then of TPC. These people included John Bloor and Peter Middleton, successively Plant Directors, as well as Bernie Carr, the late Jim Irvine, Brian Wright, Alan Hutton, Bill Wybrow, the late Alfred Tattersall, the late A. W. McCall and Mrs Rita Reynolds, who was always my initial contact when wishing to visit the works. To all these people, as well as others whose names I do not know, I owe a debt of gratitude for being so helpful and answering my many questions and thus making this book possible. Some of the above provided help or information more especially related to the later years of the Company which will be the subject of the next and final volume.

Acknowledgement is also due to Tony Kay, some of whose drawings are reproduced, and to the technical press and other publications in which references to ECW were found. I also wish to thank John Senior for his encouragement as well as Alan Townsin for converting my manuscripts into finished form in his inimitable fashion.

M. G. Doggett
Purley

United expanded its operations into County Durham within six months of the the initial 1912 venture based on Lowestoft, using a base at Cockton Hill, Bishop Auckland on which a garage and workshops were established. This Daimler Y-type, seen on a route to Durham city, was one of three placed in service in 1915. The bodybuilder is not recorded but the body style, with rear entrance and unusual in the shape of the front end of the roof, was found on several United vehicles of the period. The registration, AH 0278, followed standard Norfolk practice of the time in the inclusion of an initial zero in the number.

The first 35 years

The story of the origins and history up to 1946 of Eastern Coach Works was told in detail in my book of that title published by the Transport Publishing Company in 1987, but the following is a summary of the main strands of what was in some ways a complex sequence of events. Effectively it began with the registration of United Automobile Services Ltd on 4th April 1912 by Mr Ernest Boyd Hutchinson, the purpose being to run motor omnibus services in the vicinity of Lowestoft. The first indication that this was intended to be far more than a local bus operation came with the establishment of a branch some 250 miles to the north, at Bishop Auckland in County

Durham, in the autumn of 1912. Expansion there was quite rapid until severely curtailed by the outbreak of the First World War in August 1914. As with most other operators of motor vehicles suitable for military use, United had to give up many of its buses and indeed fifteen vehicles, about half the fleet, were lost in this way.

When the war ended in November 1918, however, the opening of new operating areas resumed and Hutchinson, very widely known by his initials E.B.H., established garaging and workshop premises in Laundry Lane, Lowestoft in 1919, expanded to include a 'car fitting shop' (where ex-military chassis were refurbished) and a 'coach

In 1919 what soon became known as the Coach Factory was established by United in Lowestoft. By the mid 'twenties, it had grown substantially, building bodies for much-modified ex-military AEC Y-type chassis in quite large numbers. An example of the style of body produced is partially visible on the right of this scene in the factory at that period.

United's operations grew rapidly and by 1926 its needs were such that 100 AEC chassis of a type built to United specification were ordered, to form the company's E class. This was the 415 model, basically an extended 413, AEC's standard single-deck model of the time, with front-end modifications to increase body space. For them, 90 saloon bodies of the type shown were built in the Coach Factory, the remainder receiving charabanc bodywork. The half-canopy styling was a United characteristic of the period, virtually unknown elsewhere. E93 had body 975.

building factory' the following year. Thus what was to become one of the most important bus bodybuilding works in the country was established, remaining on the same basic site, but greatly expanded over the years, to the end, though the address became Eastern Way in 1936.

United's areas of operation extended into Northumberland and North Yorkshire as well as East Anglia. Although it was in those days an independent concern, agreements were reached on the extent of some of the areas to be operated with both the British Electric Traction and Tilling groups, a clear indication of its growing strength. The establishment of branches in Lincolnshire and the close association with W. T. Underwood (the predecessor of East Midland Motor

Services Ltd) was further evidence of the aim to build a huge operating empire covering much of eastern England. For this purpose large fleets of new vehicles were bodied by the Coach Factory, as it was called internally, in classes of 100 or more by the late 'twenties and usually on AEC or, in 1926-28, ADC chassis. United had been one of the first purchasers of such chassis outside the Underground group (to which AEC and the London General Omnibus Co Ltd, its largest user, then belonged).

United also acted as dealers for AEC and many vehicles of this make for other operators received United bodywork up to about 1929. Indeed the Lowestoft factory built a great variety of bodywork on numerous makes of chassis for operators of many kinds including

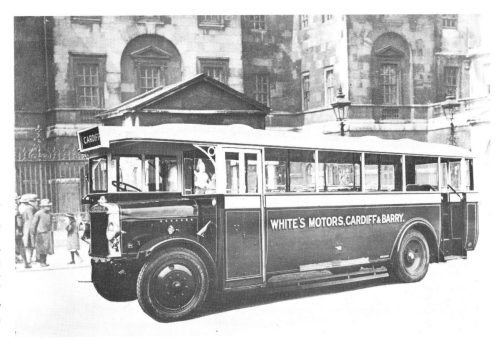

Quite different designs were built for 'outside' customers. This style was built to the requirements of the chassis maker, the Associated Daimler Co, a marketing link-up between AEC and Daimler which was in effect in the 1926-28 period. Similar bodies were also built by other bodybuilders on the 416-type chassis as shown here. This ADC photograph of an example for White's Motors of Cardiff had been given a false background of the Horse Guards building in London, added doubtless for advertising puposes. United used an oval transfer to identify its products and this is visible alongside the rear entrance step. United held an agency for AEC/ADC and was one of its main suppliers of bodywork.

By no means all of United body production was related to the company's own fleet or even the AEC/ADC connection. Leyland Motors Ltd's Nottingham branch placed an order for four coach bodies (Nos. 1795-98) of quite elaborate design on that concern's Tiger TS2 chassis, delivered in January 1929. One of them was photographed six months later by G.H.F. Atkins at Skegness – by then it was registered VO 1010 and in the fleet of G. Swain, trading as Supreme Tours, of Mansfield. The body was of quite elaborate design, described in UAS records as '50/50 saloon coach', with canvas top at the front and panelled at the rear. Another of the batch, VO 1417, owned by Ebor, is seen at the extreme left. (See also p25 of my previous volume published by TPC in 1987.)

East Midland Motor Services Ltd was a wholly-owned subsidiary of United when a batch of ten AEC Reliance models was bodied at the Coach Factory for that concern in May 1929; M2 (VO 737), with body 1883, was also seen in Skegness in July 1929. The livery – biscuit, brown and cream – was as then used by UAS itself and EMMS retained this distinctive colour scheme until the mid 'fifties, though United adopted Tilling red from 1930. The body style was also used for 130 Bristol B-type buses for United's own fleet which were in course of delivery when the concern was taken over jointly by TBAT and the LNER. In later years, Bristol chassis and bodywork built in the Lowestoft were to become a familiar combination, but there was no connection between the two concerns at that date.

municipalities and major companies, as well as smaller independents, during that period.

All that changed in June 1929 when the London & North Eastern Railway, which, like other railways at the time, was investing in bus companies, made a take-over offer. The Tilling & British Automobile Traction Co Ltd (jointly owned by Tilling and BET) made a contra-bid and the outcome was the purchase of a controlling interest by the LNER and TBAT (each holding an equal number of shares), a pattern soon to be widely repeated with bus companies elsewhere. E.B.H. resigned and a 'railway' chairman was appointed, though in later years the direction of the company and others in which the railways held interests was left to the Tilling or BET organisations, depending on which concern had the greater number of shares. Tilling thus became the dominant organisation for

United and its successors as owners of the Lowestoft coachbuilding works.

This brought the first signs of a change in status, bodywork beginning to be supplied to other companies within the wider empire of companies in which Tilling and BET held interests, though other work continued to be produced. However, United's own structure was also altered, the first indication of this being the transfer of its Lincolnshire area services to the Lincolnshire Road Car Co Ltd in January 1931. More significantly, a new company, the Eastern Counties Omnibus Co Ltd was incorporated on 14th July 1931, its function being to take over all United's activities in East Anglia, including the Coach Factory, to which were added other existing operating companies in the area also associated with Tilling or BET.

When United's Lincolnshire services were transferred to Lincolnshire Road Car Co Ltd on 1st January 1931, these ADC 415 buses of 1927 were among the vehicles handed over. The former F88 (PW 9888), nearer the camera, had become Lincolnshire AEC148 – clearly the ADC era had been forgotten by then, the vehicle being of AEC design – while F100 (PW 9900) was simply A154. The Lowestoft-built bodies (1095 and 1107) remained much as built.

Under the Eastern Counties regime, the Coach Factory became much more important as a major supplier of bodywork to associated companies than previously. This applied not only to TBAT companies but also others associated directly with Tilling on the one hand and BET on the other. Thus Eastern Counties was linked to operating companies which covered virtually every county in England and Wales and was soon to be supplying many of them with the bulk of their bus and coach body requirements. The association was always stronger on the Tilling side and, even within TBAT, there were clear policy differences, with much greater emphasis on common supply for those concerns under Tilling management, and hence wider use of Eastern Counties bodywork. Similar remarks apply to Bristol chassis, increasingly used by Tilling-controlled companies

The formation of the Eastern Counties Omnibus Co Ltd in July 1931 to take over both United's services in East Anglia and the Coach Factory was an indication of the changing circumstances which followed the transfer of United to Tilling management. Bodywork of generally similar style to that shown on Eastern Counties AT135 (NG 3879) was built for several of the associated companies in the following two years or so. This vehicle, with body 2904, was one of a batch of nine which ECOC built on Leyland Tiger TS4 chassis for its own use in March-April 1933. Leyland chassis were in quite widespread use within the Tilling-controlled companies at that time, which could be described as an interregnum between the Tilling-Stevens and Bristol periods of dominance in chassis supply to these concerns. Tyre roar from the stone setts would probably have been more evident than the sibilant sound of the Tiger's petrol engine in this scene in Huntingdon Street, Nottingham. In the background, SOS buses of the Trent company are visible.

Bristol chassis came into the picture as the products of a fellow member of the Tilling combine from 1933, though it was not until a couple of years or so later that they began to appear as the usual chassis for Lowestoft-built bodies for Tilling-controlled companies. By this date, United had become a customer rather than the direct owner of the factory, though it still held a special status as the largest shareholder in Eastern Counties. This four-cylinder petrol-engined Bristol J.NW dating from March 1935 was one of 50 supplied to form United's BJ class. Following on from them were five similar-looking vehicles on the JO5G chassis with Gardner 5LW five-cylinder oil (diesel) engine, thereafter adopted as standard for United (which classified them as BJO) and most other associated companies, and indeed the BJ class were themselves converted with 5LW engines in later years. The body style was United's standard in the mid-'thirties, being used with minor variations on Bristol and other chassis until 1938 – at that time, many major operators had their own quite distinctive single-deck body designs.

following the addition to the Tilling combine in December 1931 of the Bristol Tramways and Carriage Co Ltd (then still operating trams as well as a growing fleet of buses, in addition to making bus chassis). The combination of Bristol-built chassis and bodywork from the Coach Factory in Lowestoft was to become a familiar sight in many parts of England and Wales from the mid-'thirties, remaining a key part of the country's bus supply for nearly half a century. In the period 1936-1946, about 50 per cent of ECW's production was based on Bristol chassis but the proportion rose to some 87.2 per cent in the 'Series 2' era from 1946 to the end of production.

Body production for customers other than associated

When Eastern Coach Works Ltd was formed as a separate company in July 1936, a much more 'commercial' approach was adopted. An advertising campaign was mounted in the trade press – a new departure – and tenders put in for municipal contracts. Almost exactly a year later, the first sign of modest success appeared with the delivery of six 56-seat double-deck bodies on Leyland Titan TD5c chassis for Middlesbrough Corporation. ECW's standard highbridge double-deck design showed the influence of the arrival of Bill Bramham as General Manager from Charles H. Roe Ltd, for there were resemblences to Roe practice both in appearance and constructionally, and in addition Middlesbrough had been a Roe customer. Eagle-eyed readers may notice that the official photograph reproduced here shows the last vehicle of the batch, No. 76 (XG 5236) with body 4921, whereas a very similar view in my previous book shows No. 73, the first of the batch to be delivered. The explanation seems to be that a repeat photograph was ordered to show the completed livery – for some reason No. 73 had not received the lining out or the municipal coat of arms on the upper deck panels. Middlesbrough went on to place repeat orders for similar bodies on Titan chassis, all with the 'Gearless' torque converter transmission, the fleet of 26 such buses running most of the town's services until well into the post-war period.

companies virtually ceased during the ECOC era but when a separate company, Eastern Coach Works Ltd, was formed on 1st July 1936 to take over the Coach factory, the new management, and in particular Bill Bramham newly arrived in the company from Charles Roe's Crossgates Works at Leeds, devoted some effort to attracting other customers, notably certain municipalities, as well as increasing the scale of orders for BET-managed companies. Even so, ECW's output from the start was largely devoted to supplying the bodywork needs of the operating companies controlled by Tilling as majority shareholder. By this time, one double-deck and nine single-deck bodies on average were being produced each week by a workforce of some 950 and production remained more or less at this level, though with slightly more emphasis on double-

deckers, until well into the early months of the Second World War, declared on 3rd September 1939.

The Coach Factory was evacuated on 28th May 1940, under the threat of what was perceived as imminent invasion, but it proved possible to move to a former United Counties bus garage at Irthlingborough in Northamptonshire and ECW was able to continue bodybuilding on a very limited scale. At first, this was largely confined to completion of vehicles moved from Lowestoft, and a major part of the work done at Irthlingborough was repair and renovation of existing vehicles, largely for Tilling-controlled operating companies.

In September 1942, the TBAT group was split into quite separate parts, the difference in policy and style of

There was no such thing as a standard pre-war ECW single-deck body, for the major Tilling-controlled companies all had their own ideas, though there were often underlying similarities that could be found among the apparent variety. This example of a Bristol L5G, which was the standard single-deck chassis for such concerns from 1938, was the first of 28 for the Eastern National Omnibus Co Ltd delivered in September 1938, being ENOC's 3759 (GPU 411) with body 5856. This company favoured the half-canopy front-end, also used by North Western and Crosville, but the main body structure, with five equal-length bays ahead of the rear entrance, was similar to that favoured with full-width canopy by United Counties and East Midland. The style of waistrail, with sweeping curve downwards at the rear, was found on Crosville and United Counties saloons. The rear entrance was quite widely favoured within the Tilling-managed companies, but Crosville, West Yorkshire and, from 1939, United tended to favour the front entrance. Other companies, notably Eastern Counties and North Western, used a different body structure with 'four-and-a half' bays ahead of the entrance. The combinations of these and other features were illustrated in my previous book.

management between BET and Tilling having been such as to lead the directors to make this decision. To a large extent the Tilling line was based on the views of Sir Frederick Heaton, Chairman of Thomas Tilling Ltd from March 1931, who favoured uniformity in such matters as

vehicle design and specification controlled from the Group's London headquarters, whereas BET favoured some degree of individuality and local autonomy. The ECW concern, still a subsidiary of Eastern Counties, was included in the TBAT group companies which came into

East Yorkshire was one of the BET-controlled companies which had taken Lowestoft-built bodywork since Eastern Counties days. However, a departure in December 1938 was the supply by ECW of ten double-deck bodies which conformed to the complete British Electrical Federation design with 'Beverley Bar' Gothic roof contour as introduced for this fleet in 1934 and hitherto built for it only by Brush. Seen here at Scarborough in June 1950 is 370 (ERH 364) with body 5916, which had been rebuilt by ECW in 1947 – others of the batch were given new ECW bodies in 1948. Visible in the background is a West Yorkshire ECW-bodied L5G of similar age.

Standardisation began to become evident in ECW's double-deck production from the introduction of the Bristol K5G chassis towards the end of 1937, for which a uniform lowbridge design was to remain in production until 1940. Some variations in specification continued, however, and the total of 64 examples supplied to the North Western Road Car Co Ltd in 1938-39 were notable for the use of seating to coach standard, as also favoured in the company's single-deck buses of the period. As a result, the seating capacity was only 47, there being seats for 23 upstairs and 24 in the lower deck. Number 952 (AJA 152) had body number 6324 and was delivered in April 1939.

the 'pure Tilling' camp (though there were still railway and other minority interests). So far as its own position was concerned, this made little difference, for Tilling had already been in a dominant position in regard to United, ECOC and hence ECW, but several important users of ECW 'changed sides' as it were. New to Tilling were Crosville (though this concern had been a major user of Lowestoft-built bodywork since 1931), Lincolnshire and Cumberland, while North Western (one of the biggest customers in the 'thirties) and East Midland (despite its historic link with United) became BET subsidiaries.

Manufacture of bodywork – though at well under a tenth of its pre-war rate – was resumed at Irthlingborough, only 89 new bodies (as distinct from completion of those

begun at Lowestoft) being completed in the period from 1942 to 1945. At that time all new bus body construction was subject to the so-called 'utility' specifications laid down with Ministry of Supply authority, the objective being to economise on the use of skilled labour and scarce materials. However, rather an indulgent view was apt to be taken where new bodywork for existing chassis was to be supplied and this may partly account for the way in which these wartime ECW bodies were generally of quite well-rounded outline rather than the angular designs used for most 'utility' buses.

Most were double-deckers – 30 highbridge for the Brighton Hove & District fleet on AEC Regent chassis dating from 1931-32, and 27 lowbridge for other operators

Production of new bodies at Irthlingborough in wartime was very limited, but was significant in relation to later history, as the design of double-decker was to form the basis of subsequent ECW standards. At that time the 'utility' specifications were supposed to be enforced, but a fairly liberal attitude was apt to be taken where rebodying was concerned. The vehicle shown was the second wartime double-deck body produced, going to Wilts & Dorset Motor Services Ltd in August 1943. The chassis, a Leyland Titan TD1, had been new to Hants & Dorset in 1929 but had been sold to Wilts & Dorset in 1939, receiving a Gardner 5LW engine in the manner then common in 1942. The new body was number 8056 – although the numbering was in the same series as pre-war, there were large gaps in wartime, in some cases related to unfulfilled orders.

ECW's Lowestoft factory was vulnerable to air attack during the war, with its location in a coastal town not much over 100 miles from the nearest Luftwaffe airfields during the period when the Low Countries were occupied by the German armies. In May 1941 the factory was hit, suffering some structural damage as evident in this view, but the premises were out of use at the time. Various templates for panel shaping are visible in the foreground, one being marked 'Ribble' and hence dating from not later than 1938, when the last bodies had been built for that company.

on Leyland TD1 and TD2, AEC Regent and Bristol GO5G chassis – and conformed to the utility requirements in such aspects as five-bay construction rather than ECW's previous standard of six-bay for double-deckers, but had rounded domes and a new form of rubber glazing giving rounded corners for most windows. There were 28 single-deckers on various Tilling-Stevens, Dennis and Leyland chassis to which similar remarks applied, these further differing from the single-decker utility standard in having rear-entrance layout – as with the general appearance of the double-deckers, this was a pointer to post-war ECW and Tilling standard practice.

The first utility-style bodies to be built had been two single-deckers on new Bristol chassis with built-in gas producer plants, dating from 1942 and more in the nature of a wartime experiment (though even these had features later adopted as standard). However, two double-deckers on new Bristol K5G chassis completed in the winter of 1943-44 were true prototypes for the post-war fleet and better finished.

The Second World War came to an end in Europe on 8th May 1945 and in the Far East on 15th August that year. Even before then, the war situation had eased. The Lowestoft factory had suffered some damage in May 1941 when an enemy aircraft dropped a bomb which hit the panel shop, causing some structural damage but negligible effect on contents, for all the machinery had been removed and stored, being carefully overhauled, using parts in stock, and greased. The tight restrictions on numbers of vehicles that had been imposed at the time of the invasion scare in 1940, when no more than eight could be on the premises, were increased, allowing up to 30 in 1943 and

New single-deck bodywork built on existing chassis at Irthlingborough was even more rare than the double-deck output, but similarly gave a clue to the post-war line of development. Southern Vectis sent six Dennis Lancet chassis dating from 1934-35 for rebodying in 1944, after their return from military duties, during which time their original bodywork had deteriorated. Seen here is No. 506 (DL 9006), with new body 8359. The sharp-edged front dome was a nod in the direction of the utility requirements; otherwise, the design was functional but by no means austere, with a more rounded outline at the rear than the post-war standard.

The first of the two prototypes for the post-war ECW double-deck standard body designs to be completed was the 56-seat highbridge version, body 8063, delivered to Western National Omnibus Co Ltd as its No. 350 on 1st November 1943, though probably better known by its registration number JTA 271. Both vehicles were on a modified version of the Bristol K5G chassis, with the radiator set slightly lower than the pre-war and wartime standard and having a more rounded shape at the bottom. More important to the passengers, they had an effective flexible engine mounting system. The body outline was much the same as on those being built at Irthlingborough on reconditioned chassis at that time, and incorporated the sliding cab door adopted on the Brighton Hove & District rebodied AEC Regents. The interior was rather better finished, however, not least because of the tubular-framed seats. The interior woodwork was finished in clear varnish in wartime fashion, and by no means unattractive.

The choice of Western National as the recipient of this vehicle was somewhat surprising, as it had been a 'lowbridge' fleet in terms of regular deliveries of pre-war double-deckers and reverted to this in the post-war period. In practice, both vehicles spent much time away from their own fleets during the next year or two, and the Editor-in-Chief clearly recalls being quite impressed by a ride from Leeds to Harrogate in it when it was operating for West Yorkshire Road Car during 1944. The performance on that quite hilly route was no better than usual with the modestly powered K5G but the noise level and freedom from vibration was about on a par with a Daimler COG5, which was a great improvement on the standard K5G of the time. The body looked neat and modern both inside and out, even though the latter was in wartime dark grey.

(Bottom right) The other prototype, with 55-seat lowbridge body 8062, was completed in January 1944, the photograph being dated the 11th of that month, just under a week before it was delivered to Eastern National as that operator's 3885, registered JVW 430. In this case it was more attractively finished in green and cream, the design being much as on the highbridge version apart from the different internal layout and consequent reduced height. Visible in the offside views is the step ring, rather like that on wartime Guy models, fitted to both these buses.

were removed altogether at the end of 1944. There had been considerable evacuation from Lowestoft, and, by chance, many families were relocated in Glossop, Venture Publication's home. Some foremen returned from Irthlingborough to the Lowestoft factory at the end of January 1945 and by June nearly all who had gone to Irthlingborough five years earlier had returned, getting the factory back into shape. At first, most of the production work was on overhaul and repair, then being carried out at both locations. Irthlingborough was retained until 1952 to meet the huge demand for such work arising from enforced wartime neglect, although some new construction was also to be handled there.

The lowbridge prototype vehicle, JVW 430, is seen (left) in original condition, just before delivery to Eastern National in January 1944 and (below) as modified following its return to ECW in April 1945, after experience of periods of operation with a variety of Tilling group operators. The front destination display was altered to what became the immediate post-war group standard, with ultra-wide destination box above a combined route number and intermediate route details display – a similar unit was mounted at the rear, as shown at the foot of the page. The side route number box above the platform was painted over (though not removed, suggesting some uncertainty on the question) and a detination and route number box added over the neaside rear window. The glazing of the fixed windows below the sliders was altered to the style as used in 1946 production and the hinged vents over the front upper-deck windows removed, doubtless to improve forward vision, almost always a problem upstairs on lowbridge buses. The livery layout was altered, with upper-deck window surrounds in cream and the between-decks band carried round the front.

The lowbridge bus, JVW 430, survived almost untouched from its 1945 condition until withdrawal in 1964, when it was acquired for preservation, passing to the Eastern National Preservation Group. A full restoration is in hand as this book goes to press. The highbridge Western National bus was rebodied and was not preserved.

Body numbering methods

Serial numbers were issued to bodies from early United days and the series used remained basically the same from then until soon after the end of the war in 1945, the last new body in this series being 8811, the second in a pair of prototype post-war single-deckers.

A new series, called Series 2 (or sometimes Series II) began at 1001 for post-war production in 1946, continuing to 26600 (with some gaps) at the end of production in January 1987, and the previous numbers were retrospectively referred to as Series 1. However, there are several factors qualifying that impression of orderliness.

Serial numbers for the original manufacture of new bodies by United in 1921 began at 301, though there are records of second-hand vehicles acquired for the operating fleet being allocated lower numbers. During that era, a single series was used both for new production (for the Company's own fleet or for sale to others) and for bodies of other origins acquired new or second-hand largely from acquired businesses for the operating fleet. Service vehicles and staff cars were also included and for all of these reasons, the total output of new bodies during United ownership was considerably less than the figure suggested by what is thought to be the final United serial number (2596) issued. However, it is known that at least 1,368 new bodies were built between 1921 and 1931.

After Eastern Counties took over control, body numbers were allocated only to new bodies and continued the sequence from where United left off. When Eastern Coach Works was formed, the series continued apace and reached the early 7000s before the war interrupted new body production. However, during the war period and afterwards, numbers in this series (which became known as Series 1) were also allocated to repairs, rebuilds and renovations but with an 'R' prefix or suffix, greatly outnumbering new production at that time. Series 1 eventually reached 8903 which was allocated to the overhaul of Tyneside No. 20, a 1938 ECW-bodied Leyland Titan TD5, re-delivered on 13th October 1947. It is thought, however, that the last overhauled vehicle to leave the Coach Works was East Midland E76, a Leyland Tiger TS7, but no delivery date is shown in the records. As the wartime records are also incomplete, it is not known whether all the numbers were used for repairs, etc where gaps appear in the records, and it seems probable that some may have reflected cancellations.

The Series 2 body numbering sequence was tidier, largely because repairs and rebuilds were given a separate series and also because the uncertainties caused by the war had vanished and a much more orderly system of allocations applied through its period of use. Blanks did occur, generally due to cancelled orders or changes of plan.

A separate R series for repairs and the like began at R501 in 1951, reaching R1557 by the time the works closed. However, many repair jobs were not given serial numbers of this kind, simply being given Works or Job Numbers. Experimental bodies were given numbers in a series commencing at EX1 and continuing to EX69, though this also latterly included experimental projects and parts. There were also other series of numbers used in internal records, such as SA (Service Alterations, which included semi-warranty work, B and C which usually related to repair work, while W was Works Order numbers used for miscellaneous orders).

A general pattern in the allocation of Series 2 numbers was that they were generally batched by body type. Thus, for 1946 orders, many of which were resurrections of orders cancelled due to the war, the sequence ran – 1001-1025, lowbridge double-deck; 1026-1050, highbridge; 1051-1090, single-deck; 1091-1140, lowbridge; 1141-1167, highbridge; 1168-1235, lowbridge; 1236-1408, single-deck, all these being on new Bristol chassis. Delivery was spread from February 1946 to July 1947.

From 1947, the general pattern was that the yearly orders were batched in blocks (double-deck, single-deck and coaches, although not necessarily in that order) and often in alphabetical order of operator for each type of body. However, there were several instances where additional orders were subsequently received and further body numbers 'tacked on' to the end of those already allocated before the following year's sequence began.

The nature of the organisation, with ECW's output often going entirely or largely to associated operating companies, and very largely based on Bristol chassis also part of the same organisation meant that output could be pre-planned to a large degree. Some flexibility allowed for construction to be brought forward or deferred but the aim was always one of a fair allocation of new vehicles. Because of the batching system, vehicles leaving the works at the same time might have body numbers quite widely separated and the sequence of production was often quite far from chronological, though individual orders were almost always handled very tidily in preserving sequences of body numbers. Indeed operators' fleet and registration numbers and the chassis numbers followed a similar sequence in most cases, although of course these latter were not under the control of ECW itself.

Once the annual programme was determined, the bodies were produced in official batches, all the parts required for each batch being fabricated at the same time, and, conversely, any design change, major or minor, was reflected by a change in batch number. Thus the batch number is of significance in identifying which vehicles had particular features. This system began in 1947 with batch 1 and ended with batch 716, although the numbers 22, 23, 39, 59 and 483 were not used. The number of bodies in each batch could vary, though generally the aim was for a run of 30 to 35 bodies which was considered to be the most economical – however it could be as few as two or as many as 58. In general each batch formed part of an individual year's programme but there were many instances of the inclusion of bodies from a previous or subsequent annual programme. However, some vehicles were not included in the batch system, including one-off and other special bodies, accounting for 1,902 of those in Series 2, or 7.4 per cent of production.

Standardisation. These four designs were the Tilling group's initial post-war standard combinations of Bristol chassis with ECW bodywork, being supplied to all its bus-operating subsidiaries with minimal variation from the specifications illustrated. From left to right they were the 35-seat single-deck bus, the example being United BLO223 (HHN 223) with prototype body 8811 on Bristol L5G chassis; the 56-seat highbridge double-decker, represented by Lincolnshire 659 (DBE 185) with body 1040 on a K6A chassis; the 55-seat lowbridge body, in this case Western National 803 (HTT 974) with body 1137 on K6B chassis, and the express-service 31-seat single-decker, represented by Crosville KB1 (FFM 469) with the prototype body 8810 which had been completed in this form. The photographs are dated 22nd July 1946, the two single-deckers being the pair kept back at that time for development purposes whereas the double-deckers were early production examples photographed before delivery.

Chapter one:
The Tilling Standard era

The full effects of the September 1942 reorganisation which produced a consolidated Tilling group of operating companies did not become evident until after the war ended. Standardisation was to be carried to new levels but wartime restrictions on new vehicle production meant that this could not come into effect immediately. Indeed the fact that the Lowestoft factory was shut down because of its geographical position would have ruled out its

participation at that point. Even the adoption of two completely standardised livery styles, basically either red or green with cream relief, one or other of which was to be adopted by almost all Tilling subsidiaries, was delayed in its impact until paint supplies improved.

Eastern Coach Works was to play a key part, and indeed to gain considerable benefit in terms of simplified production, from the new regime. There was to be one design of each type of body and only one – gone were the days when each major operator had its own characteristic outline of saloon body – and all details right down to such items as destination displays and upholstery moquette (one design which cleverly incorporated reds and greens so as to match either standard livery) were to conform to the pattern. Within the Tilling group, this system was to be applied with great rigidity, aided by similar standardisation on Bristol chassis.

It was not possible to be so firm on detail requirements with other customers, mainly BET companies and certain municipal fleets, who either had orders outstanding at the end of the war or placed fresh orders. However, even for them ECW was not prepared to build bodywork which did not conform to one or other of the standard designs in outline and layout. Other bodybuilders were also often less accommodating than they had been up to 1939, but ECW was unusually firm in its policy. In the circumstances of the times, with a huge backlog of unfulfilled demand to meet, it was a logical if rather harsh course of action and helped to maximise output when it was most needed.

There were to be lowbridge and highbridge double-deckers, each derived from, and quite closely resembling, the two prototype buses built for Eastern National and Western National in 1943-44, and based on the Bristol K-type chassis as standard. This now had the lower-mounted PV2-type radiator and was to be available in K5G, K6A or K6B forms with Gardner 5LW five-cylinder or either AEC 7.7-litre or Bristol AVW six-cylinder engines respectively. All of these could be accommodated within the standard bonnet length and thus did not affect body dimensions – Bristol also supplied the K6G with the longer Gardner 6LW unit for other operators but it was not offered at that stage with ECW bodywork.

Both double-deck body designs were of rear-entrance layout, this being almost universal among British fleets in general at that time, and usually seated 55 in lowbridge form with sunken side gangway on the upper deck (27 seats upstairs and 28 down) and 56 (30 up, 26 down) in the centre-gangway highbridge form. The lowbridge design was the more widely favoured by Tilling companies, many of which standardised on the type in a way characteristic of the group, even for routes where headroom would permit the taller highbridge buses, and despite the latter's advantages in comfort and ease of circulation for passengers and conductor.

Similarly there was to be only one single-deck outline, also with rear entrance (previously Tilling companies had been somewhat divided in this respect, with United and West Yorkshire among prominent users favouring the front entrance in 1939). Usually seating was provided for 35 passengers, but there was also to be an 'express' version with more luxurious seats for 31 and a livery with more extensive use of cream, as standardised for use by

This ECW official photograph is believed to show the first of the two prototype post-war single-deck bodies in a part-complete state. The exact date is not known, but the two chassis were delivered on 22nd December 1945 and the negative number indicates that it was taken before the views of the first production double-decker, which was delivered on 22nd February 1946. It is possible to discern the stub starting-handle shaft of an AEC engine on the original print, and thus it appears that this is the first of the pair, chassis W4.001, which was an L6A and received body 8810, later becoming Crosville KB1 (FFM 469). Though lacking seats and various body fittings, it had been glazed, and it is noteworthy that the offside had no opening windows whereas the nearside had the square-cornered sliding vents above fixed windows with radiused corners, as used in early production – it seems possible that already there were doubts about the appearance of the latter. Noteworthy, however, is the way in which the outline and styling contours were exactly as put into production – ECW designs of that period had the sureness of touch of the true artist. It was in bus-style livery as seen here but body 8810 was completed by about May 1946 as the prototype 'express' version of this body design, as shown on page 27.

Production restarted at Lowestoft with the delivery of the first batch of buses to the standard post-war designs to leave the factory. Above is seen body 1001 of Series 2, the first in the new sequence, which was of the 55-seat lowbridge design, the first of a batch on Bristol K6A chassis for Crosville, this one being MB251 in that fleet, registered FFM 432, delivered on 22nd February 1946. The design quite closely resembled the 1944 prototype built for Eastern National, particularly as rebuilt in 1945 and shown on page 20, but it is noteworthy that the hinged vents over the front upper-deck windows had reappeared. In addition, the bold decision had been taken to repeat the very large front destination display not only at the rear but also on the side, despite the need to modify the body framing to accomodate it. The PV2 radiator on the Bristol chassis, henceforth to be standard on all subsequent types with exposed radiator, was lowered more noticeably than on the prototypes and shaped differently at the bottom. The AEC 7.7-litre engine tended to be favoured by operators where six-cylinder Leylands had been standard hitherto; it could be identified by the projecting starting handle shaft and the higher access hole in the bonnet side, though the latter was also used with the Bristol engine, quite rare at first. Unladen weight, at 7tons 6cwt, was rather more than half-a-ton greater than pre-war equivalents.

The line-up of the first batch of eight vehicles, with body numbers 1001-8, outside the Lowestoft factory made a brave sight on a rather gloomy February day in 1946 after the long wartime spell when the place had been used for the manufacture of wartime camouflage netting. At that stage, the livery was still to the layout used on the prototype in 1945 form, with cream surround to the upper-deck front windows. Nearest the camera is FFM 434, Crosville MB253.

Comparison of the upper-deck interiors of the 1944 prototype and early post-war production lowbridge bodies underlines the relationship as well as the way the origin lies in ECW's interpretation of the wartime utility specification. This view shows Eastern National 3885 (JVW 430) with body 8062 in its slightly modified form after returning to ECW in 1945. As a prototype, it was allowed to have better seats than usual at that date, and the style of frame, with built-in hand rail, suggests a touch of the London Transport RT influence also evident in the sliding cab door and lowering of the radiator shown in other views (RT19 had visited Brighton Hove & District, which had good links to Tilling headquarters, in its wartime demonstration tour). In other respects it was a little austere, with no interior linings to the roof or side panels, though this had been quite common pre-war, when weight restrictions made single-skin roof panels quite usual and side trim was apt to be omitted on the upper deck.

The early post-war ECW production bodies as built in 1946-7 had seats which were a little inferior to those of the prototype in not being of the tubular-framed type and lacking top rails. They were trimmed in moquette using the Tilling group's ingenious and attractive pattern using a mixture of red, green and grey which was standard in both 'red' and 'green' Tilling fleets. A similar style was used for the side lining, and the roof was double skin. The identity of the vehicle is not certain – the standardisation was such that any lowbridge body built for a Tilling fleet in 1946 looked the same – but it is thought to be body 1110 on Thames Valley 440 (CRX 549), a K6A of which other official views were taken.

the Tilling companies. This was to be ECW's closest approach to a coach, as generally understood, until 1950. Again the Bristol chassis was to be standard, in this case the L-type, the single-deck equivalent to the K, similarly updated and with the same engine options.

Two prototype bodies of the new single-deck design were built, the exact date of completion not being known, though circumstantial evidence suggests that at least one had been taken to the stage of being a running prototype by quite early in 1946. The L-type chassis had the same new style of PV2 radiator, bonnet etc as had been introduced for the double-deckers and had chassis numbers W4.001 and W4.002, indicating that they were the first in Bristol's fourth wartime series of sanctions (the double-deck K-

type equivalent was the W3 series, of which the first examples received utility bodywork by Duple or Strachans, beginning to reach operators from December 1945). The use of the W prefix suggests that authorisation for the construction of chassis in these sanctions was given before the war ended, and these first two examples were delivered to ECW on 22nd December 1945.

The new single-deck body design was clearly in many ways a direct equivalent of the double-deck version, with similar pillar spacing, glazing and cab design. There were some resemblances to the small numbers of wartime single-deck bodies built at Irthlingborough, but there were also clear indications of an endeavour to make a decisive step forward. The body sides were continued

upward by about 1ft. above the saloon window line before curving inwards in a smaller-radius curve than usual in a bus roof of that period. This idea had been found in a milder form on some pre-war ECW saloon bodies, where advertising panels had been provided above the windows (notably for Eastern Counties, but also in the BET Federation design) but the post-war ECW single-deckers integrated it into the body design to a degree not seen before. This had logical justification in that it made the internal luggage racks above the seats (standard on nearly all single-deckers for Tilling-managed companies since the mid-'thirties) more roomy as well as, externally, providing a useful space for advertisements if carried, thus allowing them to look much tidier than if stuck on panels not providing an appropriate-looking space.

The other major feature of the design was the inclusion of the same type of very large destination indicator panel

The exact dates when the two prototype single-deckers for the post-war standard range were completed are not recorded, but appear to have been about May 1946, two months or so before series delivery of the bus version began. This photograph shows the second one, body 8811, built for United on Bristol L5G chassis W4.002, posed for its official photographs – note the use of a set of Eastern Counties destination blinds borrowed for the occasion, no doubt to assess the overall effect on a design where so much emphasis had been set on route information.

The vehicle had been given its United fleet number BLO223 and registration HHN 223, though the post-war production deliveries of similar buses were to begin at BLO143 in July. The initial order for 80 for United was not completed until 1947, the prototype thus 'following on'. It was not delivered until February 1947, being used initially as a development vehicle. The incorporation of such massive destination screens at the rear of a single-decker set problems for the designer, yet the overall appearance was very neat, similar remarks applying to the treatment of the external sliding door. The doors at the rear gave access to a luggage locker, but this was much shallower than the depth of the opening suggested, due to the intrusion of the space occupied by the rear seat.

The other single-deck prototype, with body 8810, was similarly photographed with borrowed destination blinds soon afterwards in the Spring of 1946. It had been completed to the 'express' specification, with coach seats for 31 passengers, Crosville KB1 (FFM 469) was not delivered until January 1947, and even then was to remain the only example of this version of Tilling standard design for a while.

The interior of the standard single-deck bus as built for the Tilling group in its initial 1946 form was neatly executed. This view shows how it looked from the rearmost seat, a position not infrequently taken by the conductor when the vehicle was not full. The seats were rather more austere than those normally found in bodies built for Tilling-controlled companies in the late 'thirties, with comparatively low backs, but the overall effect was both practical and 'welcoming' in a way by no means always achieved nearly half a century later. The overhead luggage racks were quite capacious because of the roof contour. The vehicle shown is the United prototype, BLO223, with body 8811, but production vehicles followed the same design.

at front and rear that had been incorporated in the 1944 prototype lowbridge double-deck body (Eastern National 3885) after its return to ECW for modifications in April 1945. This was probably the largest area of display for destination, route number and 'via' details used on a single-decker anywhere in Britain (even London Transport reduced its normal destination display considerably when applied to single-deckers). The front box was neatly faired into the body, though projecting well above the roof line, and at the rear the window was squared off at a level similar to the side windows to accommodate it.

The rear entrance door was of the external sliding type, but neatly fitted into the body outline in such a way as to largely avoid the untidy effect often given when a sliding door was not arranged to disappear behind the panelling when open. Overall both the double- and single-deck versions of the new 'Tilling standards' had a 'clean' functional look and, despite their derivation from what were admittedly very liberal interpretations of wartime utility designs, smooth and modern-looking in a way which caught the feeling of a new age in the hopeful, if still difficult, post-war world. It could be argued that they had as powerful an impact on bus design as the London RT double-decker, sharing with that model an ability to make many other styles of the period look rather dated.

The two prototype single-deckers, with Series 1 body numbers 8810 and 8811, were eventually delivered to the Crosville and United fleets but not until 3rd January and 3rd February 1947, respectively, by which time nearly 100 of the production version of the new single-decker had been completed. It is thought that the two had been retained by ECW for development purposes, 8810 eventually being completed to 31-seat express specification, acting as prototype for that variation, while 8811 was finished to 35-seat bus form.

The first post-war production vehicles to be completed were double-deckers, and it is significant that there was a

(continued on page 31)

Despite the generally strict standardisation, minor variations were to be found. After the first fifteen lowbridge bodies, an additional opening window was added at the centre of each side of the lower deck, this variation applying to the next 35 (body numbers 1016-25 and 1091-1115), as shown here on 1110, supplied to Thames Valley as No. 440 (CRX 549). This view also shows the standard Tilling livery style in the form that was adopted for double-deckers from this period right through to the mid 'sixties, with cream bands, edged in black, at between-decks and upper-deck waist levels. Realisation that sliding vents offered less opening area than the half-drops more usual in pre-war days led to a further change, when a continuous row of five opening windows on each side of the upper deck, as well as the three downstairs, was adopted. These were still of the square-cornered type through the remaining 1946 and early 1947 lowbridge batches (1116-40, 1168-1210); a further pair of bodies supplied to Eastern Counties (1226-7) also had square-cornered sliders but of a different type made by Beclawat. The sliding cab door of the prototypes had given way to a conventional hinged design from the beginning of production.

Anyone observing deliveries from ECW during 1946 might have thought that the pre-war standard designs of double-decker were still available, as Western Welsh received thirteen examples on new AEC Regent II chassis of bodywork to the outlines that had been familiar in 1937-40. As explained more fully in my previous volume, however, these were built up from sets of parts that had been stored since 1940, when they had been intended for the balance of an order for fifteen, of which only two chassis were delivered. The post-war deliveries comprised six lowbridge, including body 7200, Western Welsh 617 (CKG 797) seen here before delivery in May 1946, and seven highbridge. The contrast in body style between the two generations of design is self-evident, though several other bodybuilders were still producing new bodywork to virtually pre-war designs of comparable appearance at the time save perhaps that six-bay construction had become rare. The 'British Buses' emblems and slogan were part of a public relations campaign being run by BET group (to which Western Welsh belonged) and certain other operators at the time, largely as a defence against what was seen as the threat of nationalisation.

The highbridge version of the standard double-deck body had a slightly 'softer' outline, due to the more rounded roof contours. The provision of sliding windows was to the more generous standard, with five on each side of the upper deck and three below on all the bodies of this type built to the 1946 specification with square-cornered sliding vents (1026-50 and 1141-53) — all but three were delivered before the end of the year. Seen here in Lincoln in August 1946 is Lincolnshire 662 (DBE 188), a K6A with body 1043. This was a company that had only a handful of double-deckers pre-war but was expanding its intake like many other of the more rural fleets to meet the need for more high-capacity buses. The clarity of lettering possible with the wide destination display is notewothy, though the 'via' screen has begun to roll slightly crooked, which was a problem with this design.

The immediate post-war production standard ECW single-deck body on Bristol L-type chassis was almost identical to the prototype – seen here is body 1054, the fourth of the first series 1051-90; 1236-77 were similar. This was United BLO144 (GHN 944), an L5G which entered service early in July 1946, photographed at Scarborough four years later. Again, the destination display sets a standard of readability rarely if ever exceeded at any period before or since. Almost all the vehicles concerned were completed to Tilling specification, the body numbers being allocated to the various operating companies in quite small batches, possibly because of the continuation of the wartime allocation system for orders in hand prior to the Spring of 1946.

Intermingled with the 1946 deliveries of single-deckers on Bristol L-type chassis to Tilling companies were seven with non-standard details for Welsh municipal fleets (four to Aberdare Urban District Council and three to Merthyr Tydfil Corporation), both established users of Bristol chassis but not ECW bodywork. Four were on L6A chassis for Aberdare (body numbers 1083-4, 1250 and 1320). Three of these were within the 'square-cornered sliding vent' group but body 1320, seen here on Aberdare 26 (FTX 479) built in 1947, is shown also to have this 'early' feature, although numbered well into the sequence having the later type in terms of main production for Tilling fleets – a similar pattern was evident in bodies built for BET and other companies. Visible behind it is Aberdare No. 31 (ETX 706), a 1942 Bristol L5G with East Lancs body.

A remarkable feature of the Aberdare vehicles is that they had wooden seats, of the slatted type as found on wartime utility buses of around 1943-44, something which ECW had managed to avoid producing because of its concentration on rebodying for its small wartime production programme. The reasoning was that wooden seats were more suitable for coal miners returning home from work in the days before pithead baths, when their clothing would make upholstery dirty and difficult to clean. This requirement persisted on to a further four L6A buses built later in 1947 and having the later type of opening windows. Seen here is body 2212, on Aberdare 32 (GTG 870), though renumbered 36 in 1958. They also lacked the luggage racks standard on Tilling examples and this reveals the straight-sided roof cross-section.

An order for 80 bus bodies for Western Welsh on the newly-introduced Leyland Tiger PS1 chassis was met by supplying a design which differed only slightly from the contemporary ECW standard, including the rear entrance position, virtually unknown for a single-decker in that fleet. The different chassis required a modified cab design with wider but shallower windscreen, with horizontal lower edge. The operator specified the Clayton indicator, widely favoured in BET companies, and the livery treatment was different. Deliveries of the order (bodies 1493-1572) began in 1946, continuing to mid-1947, but the square-cornered window vents remained standard for the batch. Seen here is Western Welsh 858 (CUH 858) with body 1553. A feature not visible in this view is the use of a divided rear window, which was associated with ECW bus bodies on PS1 chassis generally, though evidently simply by association with the Western Welsh specification rather than for any reason related to the type of chassis.

A modified type of sliding vent, designed by ECW to fit within the rubber glazing of the full-depth main window aperture, was adopted part-way through the 1946 programme, though deliveries of the new design generally began in the earlier part of 1947. This example on an L5G chassis, United BLO185 (GHN 985), with body 1452, delivered in May of that year, is of additional interest in having been built at Irthlingborough, and having the slightly higher mounting of the front registration plate associated with examples built there. By the time the photograph was taken, its side destination box had been replaced by an additional opening window, just in front of the entrance. Irthlingborough construction of L-type bodies began in February 1947, at first with square-type sliding vents.

pronounced shift from the split of output in the period from 1936 to when output was virtually cut-off by the war in 1940, when the proportion of double-deckers was about a quarter of the total. It rose comparatively slightly in 1946, but in the succeeding years of the late 'forties, double-deckers were in the majority, with a high point of 69.5% of bodies produced against the 1948 production programme of 1062 units of which 738 were double-deck, although of course many were not delivered until the following year.

It is noteworthy that the workforce employed at Lowestoft, at approximately 1,300, was 300 more than before the war, and it is a measure of improved production methods and the benefits of standardisation that this modest increase was proportionately far less than that in output, which more than doubled despite the higher proportion of double-deckers. There were also another 160 staff at Irthlingborough, but they were largely employed on overhaul and repair work rather than new vehicle build.

The fresh start was signified by the beginning of the new sequence of body numbers at 1001, this being the start of Series 2, the first batches covering 25 lowbridge followed by 25 highbridge double-deckers and then 40 single-deckers before another run of 50 lowbridge and so on, as explained in the note on body numbering methods.

Construction tended not to be in strict numerical order, however, and as time went on this became increasingly evident as the allocations of numbers became more in the nature of a programme usually compiled annually and in advance while the actual order build was related to practical factors.

The standard body designs were adaptable with minor changes to other makes of chassis, the first variation to arise, during 1946, being the Leyland Tiger PS1, of which 80 had been ordered by Western Welsh, who had been a customer for earlier types of Tiger with front-entrance ECW bodywork to the BET Federation design in pre-war days. Doubtless this would have been preferred again, in line with several other BET group operators who took delivery of PS1 chassis with Federation bodywork constructed by other builders in the early post-war days, but only quite minor changes to the ECW standard rear-entrance design were incorporated. The different chassis, with bonnet slightly longer as well as taller than on the post-war Bristol, required adjustments to the body design to accommodate it. What was basically the same body structure in 'express' 31-seat form was adapted to meet a demand from Southdown Motor Services Ltd – not previously an ECW customer – for coaches, some 25 such vehicles being supplied in the earlier part of 1947.

Before the standard Tilling group express 31-seat version of the standard single-deck design went into production, Southdown Motor Services Ltd placed what amounted to a close derivative of the design in service, based on Leyland Tiger PS1 chassis. Hitherto, Southdown had not been an ECW customer, despite having been within the same TBAT combine in pre-war days, yet somewhat ironically became one, despite being by then a BET company, in the post-war era. It had urgent need for new coaches and spread its orders for bodywork much wider than hitherto, though specifying rear-entrance layout and usually 32-seat capacity, as had applied with previous generations of Tiger coaches back to 1930. The ECW design was judged a close enough approach to this concept, though more angular in lines and with seats for 31 passengers, so 25 were ordered, receiving ECW body numbers 1636-60 and delivered as Southdown 1227-51 (not in the same order) between February and May 1947. Most features of the ECW design were accepted, including the waistline mouldings, though with Southdown's coach-style front destination display and side route boards. However, there seems to have been some unease about the opening windows from early on. Some, at least, entered service with the then new ECW standard sliding vents (there being photographic evidence of body 1644 at Victoria thus) but body 1638 had much deeper sliding vents while 1640 (Southdown 1246) had full-depth sliding windows as built, as shown in the accompanying three-quarter rear view which appears to show it on return to ECW after a period in service — unusually for Southdown it had collected a few dents. All of these options were considered unsatisfactory, and special half-drop windows conforming to the ECW outline were fitted within a few months, as shown by the top view of Southdown 1240 (body 1648) in service at Victoria in 1950.

The revised type of opening windows came in for the latter part of the 1946 programme, appearing on single-deck bus bodies 1278-1408 and 1416-63, largely delivered in the earlier part of 1947. The same type of body in the 1947 programme, of which deliveries began in July 1947, spilling over well through 1948 (1915-2125 and 2180-9), incorporated a further change, the rear registration number being displayed on a translucent plate above slightly shallower boot doors. Generally, appearance did not change in other respects, though body 1966, delivered in January 1948 and shown here on Eastern Counties LL668, on L5G chassis, had an experimental rear entrance door, sliding within the rearmost side window panel which thus became flush with the body side — marginally neater but not adopted as standard. By this time the batch system had begun, bodies 1915-2125 being in batches 13-16 (though some of them included bodies in the 1948 programme), while 2180-9 formed part of batch 18, largely composed of 'express' type 31-seaters and emphasising the close affinity between bus and express versions.

Most of the 1947 double-deck programme was very tidy, with 55-seat lowbridge bodies on Bristol K-type chassis (1589-1635 and 1661-1804) forming batches 1 to 7, built between August 1947 and July 1948. The design was quite standardised, with eight of the new-style opening windows on each side, body 1742, United Counties 640 (DBD 981) on K5G chassis shown here being typical. Included with this programme was the first instance of rebodying using this design, body 2204, forming part of batch 7, being mounted on Western National No. 316. This was a 1940 K5G damaged by fire, the chassis receiving a PV2 radiator and thus looking much the same as the new examples.

The lower-deck interior of a typical 1947-48 lowbridge body to Tilling standard specification had obvious similarities to that of the single-decker, though perhaps slightly less stylish. At this stage composite construction was still being used and the sides were thicker than applied later, though the revised windows looked tidier within as well as from outside. At the front, Bristol's continued use of the external Autovac fuel feed system. mounted relatively high on the dash panel, caused an obstruction to the nearside front passenger's vision and similar remarks applied to a lesser degree to the switchbox to the right of the driver's seat. At this stage, Bristol was still using rigid engine mountings, so the noise and vibration level with the Gardner 5LW engine in a K5G in particular was high and if the hinged vent in the bulkhead window was opened the noise became even greater. The K6A and K6B were rather smoother but certainly not quiet, similar remarks applying to the single-deck equivalents.

An unusually low bridge in Leeman Road, York resulted in ten L5G single-deckers with bodies 2116-25 for the York-West Yorkshire fleet having front destination boxes of modified shape to reduce the overall height from the usual 10ft. 2in. to 9ft. 8½in. The upper 'destination' blind was omitted, and a corresponding change was made at the rear even though that did not involve any reduction in height. They were built as parts of batches 12 and 13, delivery being between August 1947 and March 1948. Seen here in service some years later is Y242 (FWX 817), the front blind aperture having been further reduced by internal masking.

Most of the 1947 series of highbridge bodies were standard Tilling group vehicles on Bristol K chassis (1805-1914 in batches 8-11), but in the first three months of the year nine AEC Regent II double-deckers were bodied in similar style, apart from seats, indicator display etc. for the local Lowestoft Corporation fleet with bodies numbered 1579-87 – No. 21 (GBJ 192) with body 1581 being shown. A tenth body of similar design (1588) was built on the same type of chassis for the Ebor Bus Co Ltd in February as its No. 21 (HAL 841) but this business passed to Mansfield & District in 1950 and the vehicle became the latter's No. 118. The Regent II chassis had a higher bonnet line than the post-war Bristol K but apart from accomodating this the body was almost identical in design. Another municipal order for highbridge bodies was for Aberdare but these (2205-9), delivered in November, were on Bristol K6A chassis.

East Yorkshire took three similar-bodied PS1 coaches in December 1947.

Similar remarks applied to subsequent orders for bodywork on various models of new AEC and Leyland chassis as well as to the rebodying of pre-war chassis of varying makes and models, several Tilling and BET companies being involved in programmes of this kind.

The Tilling-controlled companies had followed a similar policy in pre-war days, continuing into the 'fifties, but BET's involvement was more of a change. The first post-war instance of a new ECW body on an existing chassis was in May 1947, when Western National 316, a Bristol K5G of 1940 reappeared with new lowbridge body number 2204 after a fire, but large-scale programmes began in 1948.

The main activity was, however, to begin the huge task of meeting the demand for new vehicles for the Tilling companies. These had long followed a policy of extending the lives of old vehicles but there was much overdue replacement to be done as well as fleet expansion to meet growing demand for travel, many of the fleets having received only small numbers of new vehicles during the war. These had been of unsatisfactory design, particularly in regard to the utility bodywork with its austere design and often poor-quality timber in its framework. This last factor was a problem in regard to new construction, supplies of good-quality hardwood being very poor in the early post-war years, which affected ECW as well as other builders who were still using what was generally called composite construction, based on timber framing, with panelling usually in aluminium alloy.

Bristol chassis production was also expanded but could not meet all the demands put on it. However, the Tilling group found that Leyland could supply 150 of its

The North Western Road Car Co Ltd had been one of ECW's biggest users in pre-war days, and its switch to the BET group in 1942 had caused widespread surprise. In the early post-war period, the momentum of earlier days lived on, with 25 Bristol L5G having ECW bodywork in 1946 (1464-88), followed by 32 in the latter part of 1947 (2136-67, forming batch 17, of which body 2154 on No. 179 is seen here). These were largely to the standard ECW design with the usual 35-seat capacity, but North Western exerted its new position to specify seats a little nearer its pre-war standard, higher-backed than the Tilling pattern, and also a single destination display at the front. The red and white livery was to NWRCC style, but the uninitiated might well have thought that this was still a Tilling-controlled company, especially as a batch of ten ECW-bodied lowbridge Leyland PD1 buses very similar to those supplied to several Tilling fleets also entered service in 1948.

Delivery of the 100 Leyland Titan PD1 (or to be precise, PD1A, with Metalastik shackle pins) bodied as lowbridge by ECW (2214-2313, in batches 19 to 21) for Tilling companies began in June 1947 and continued until the following March. The design differed from the version for Bristol chassis because the Leyland bonnet was longer as well as higher than that of the K-type. The front profile was altered, the driver's windscreen being inclined more strongly as well as being shallower but wider, extending to the centre-line of the body and having a horizontal lower edge to suit the front dash supplied with the chassis. In addition the front bay of the main body structure was shortened slightly, and this meant that the standard sliding-vent opening window could not be fitted in this position on the upper deck. Seating capacity was 53, that in the lower deck being reduced to 26 instead of the Tilling group's usual 28. Crosville received the largest share, 35 vehicles, the others being divided between Eastern Counties (20), Eastern National (18), Western National (12), Hants & Dorset (7), Southern National (4) and Lincolnshire (4). The last-mentioned's 691 (DFW 568), new in January 1948, is seen in Skegness in July 1949.

A further 25 PD1A were bodied as highbridge (2314-38) for operation by Bristol and delivered during the winter of 1947-48. The body design was similarly modified though in this case the 56-seat capacity was not altered since the 26-seat lower deck was standard. As usual with Bristol, the destination display did not conform to the Tilling standard, BTCC using a single all-purpose screen at the front which was narrower but of approximately similar depth as built. However, by the time C4017 (KHW 628) was photographed in Old Market Street, Bristol, in April 1960, the depth used had been reduced by masking in the way quite common as operators began to economise on destination displays as part of an effort to contain costs.

Titan PD1 double-deck chassis relatively quickly. Of these, 100 were fitted with ECW lowbridge bodywork and split between seven of the operating companies. The remaining 50 were allocated to the operational department of the Bristol Tramways & Carriage Co Ltd – a case of 'coals to Newcastle' – and 25 of these received ECW highbridge bodywork, the remainder being fitted with bodies of similar specification built in BTCC's own bodyshops (17) and by a local concern, Longwell Green Coachworks (8).

Various other orders for operators outside the Tilling group were also built in the early post-war period. The North Western Road Car Co Ltd, by now part of the BET

group, might almost have been thought to still belong to the Tilling empire, with batches of 25 and then 32 Bristol L5G models, followed by ten Leyland PD1 lowbridge double-deckers, all with ECW bodywork of standard outline, though with non-Tilling details in regard to seats, indicators and finish. Two Welsh municipal operators, Aberdare and Merthyr Tydfil, which had favoured Bristol chassis before the war, placed small post-war orders for L-types, but with ECW bodywork for the first time, the former also taking highbridge K-type double-deckers. Lowestoft Corporation placed what amounted to a repeat order for highbridge double-deckers on AEC Regent chassis, although the previous eight, very different in

Deliveries of the production version of the 'express' 31-seat body on Bristol L chassis did not begin until September 1947, when Lincolnshire began receiving a batch of four (2200-3), including 686 (DFW 358) with body 2201 seen here, and very few of the type were to be seen until 1948. The L6B chassis, with Bristol AVW engine, was widely favoured for this body style, as here, and the combination seemed well-suited to medium-distance express services. The 1947 programme also included twelve for Bristol's own fleet (2168-79), and ten each for West Yorkshire (2126-35) and Eastern National (2190-9), the last-mentioned being on L5G chassis,

The only examples of AEC Mark III passenger chassis to receive ECW bodywork from new were four Regal models which received a slightly modified version of the standard 35-seat body (2356-9) for the Londonderry and Lough Swilly Railway. The lines of the body suited those of the chassis, with its sloping bonnet line, quite well, as can be seen in the AEC official photograph taken at Southall before shipment in February 1948. The chassis were of the O682 type, with 7.7-litre engine and crash gearbox as had been used in the Regent II etc. The later in-service view below shows not only a modified livery but the roof luggage container, evidently added after arrival, though the rear window had been provided with a broad central division in which steps were fitted.

design and dating from 1931, had been built at almost the end of the days when United had been the proprietors of the Coach Factory. This time there were nine on the Regent II chassis, delivered early in 1947, one further basically similar bus going to an independent operator, the Ebor Bus Co Ltd of Mansfield. However, the latter was not quite the first independent operator to receive a new ECW-bodied vehicle (none had been built for an operator in this category pre-war, nor, indeed by the Coach Factory since United days, in 1931). Birch Bros of Kentish Town, London, took six Leyland Tiger PS1 buses of similar general design to the Western Welsh batch, one being delivered before the end of 1946 and the rest in 1947. A further six in early autumn 1948 had coach seats.

Other noteworthy orders fulfilled in that period included one delivered in February 1948 from the Londonderry and Lough Swilly Railway for four 35-seat saloon bodies on AEC Regal III chassis, unique as the only new Mark III

series AEC chassis bodied by ECW, and also for this pattern of body in having a roof-mounted luggage container, still widely favoured in both Northern Ireland and Eire. Four Leyland Tiger PS1 buses for Isle of Man Road Services Ltd were another instance of ECW products

Quite a promising trade in rebodying Leyland Titan models of the late 'thirties for BET companies arose in the post-war period, when the original bodywork on many such vehicles was getting beyond economic repair yet the chassis were highly regarded and fit for many more years of service. ECW secured substantial business of this type, carrying it out in 1948, and might well have obtained more had not 'politics' intervened. The first orders to go through were lowbridge bodies, 24 for East Kent, not hitherto an ECW customer, (2410-33) and 25 for Ribble, which had been quite a big ECW buyer in 1936-8, (2434-58), all delivered between May and July 1948. Neither these nor the other rebodying orders for BET companies were given batch numbers. The standard lowbridge body design fitted well on the TD4 chassis, used for all but four of the East Kent vehicles, and the dimensionally-identical TD5 of the remainder as well as the Ribble order, with no more than minor adjustments to suit the mildly higher bonnet line. It is noteworthy that the East Kent batch had aluminium main pillars, the first recorded instance of use of aluminium framing in production ECW bodies for home market customers, though its use was soon to become usual. The five main bays were of standard length and sliding vents could be fitted in all five places on the upper deck, though Ribble chose not to do so.

Seen here are East Kent JG 8231, a TD4 of 1937, with body 2420 at Folkestone in July 1952, and Ribble 1803 (RN 8187), a TD5 new in 1938 and photographed just before leaving ECW with body 2435 ten years later – it was to give a further eleven years of service before withdrawal. The standard post-war Ribble front destination glass shape had given a little trouble to the installer of the usual delivery publicity poster because of its shape; the upper part incorporated a three-track number blind.

shipped in a similar direction, even if only part way across the Irish Sea.

An unusual and significant order came from the Red & White group, then still independent, for 25 lowbridge bodies on Albion Venturer CX19 chassis, of which eight went to United Welsh and the remainder to the main Red & White fleet, all delivered in July-August 1948.

There were instances of variations in specification even within the Tilling group, such as Bristol Tramways single-deck buses with doorways at front and rear, and the Brighton livery that had been agreed as applying to both Brighton Hove & District and the municipal buses in that town.

The problem of an adequate supply of good-quality hardwood has already been mentioned, but ECW was

carrying out development work on a fresh approach to body construction. Some very successful metal-framed designs from other bodybuilders had been in production since the 'thirties but most of these were based on steel framing. Various firms had tried the use of aluminium alloy as a material for body framing (it was already in almost universal use for panelling) without a great deal of success, but it had important potential advantages in weight-saving and relative freedom from the problem of corrosion which afflicted some steel-framed designs.

An opportunity to put this work to use came when an export order from South Africa was obtained. There were strong pressures from the Government to seek export orders to help to reduce the immense outflow of national funds that had occurred due to the war. Raw material

East Yorkshire Motor Services Ltd was, like Ribble, a former ECW user. Indeed, all but one of the fifteen new double-deck bodies supplied in October-November 1948 replaced ECW products of 1938-39 originally carried from new by the Leyland TD5 chassis involved – a similar body rebuilt rather than replaced is seen on page 16. All were to this operator's characteristic 'Beverley Bar' roof contour, permiting centre-gangway highbridge bodies to pass through the gothic arch in that town which lay on several of the company's routes. In other respects, the new bodies conformed to the ECW highbridge standard outline, and were fitted with destination indicators of Clayton pattern with 'flipover' boards to allow rapid alteration at the end of the route without altering the main screen – the front one on 382 (GAT 68), seen here with body 2473 at Scarborough in July 1950, is in the up position while that on the side indicator box is down. The vehicle had been new in December 1939 and although it was withdrawn in 1956 along with the rest of the rebodied examples, it was one of several which remained in passenger-carrying service with various independent operators for some years subsequently – in this case running for Smith's of Reading in 1957-62.

Orthodox highbridge bodies were also built as part of the rebodying exercise being carried out by some BET companies. The Northern General Transport Co Ltd had not so far been an ECW customer, though one of its subsidiaries, the Tyneside Tramways and Tramroads Co, had taken eight ECW-bodied Leyland Titan TD5 buses in 1938. The more usual double-deck body supplier to NGT and its subsidiaries at that time was Weymann, and both NGT itself and the Tynemouth and District Transport Co Ltd took TD5 models thus bodied earlier that year. They were metal-framed and such bodies generally had long lives, but it may have been the effect of the large opening for the front entrance that had been specified that led to the decision to rebody them. All five of the Northern batch received new ECW bodies (2474-8) and similarly all eight of the Tynemouth buses were fitted with ECW bodies 2973-80 to the same specification, delivery of both occurring between October and December 1948. The big gap in body numbers reflects the fact that the Tynemouth buses were regarded as part of the 1948 rather than 1947 programme as had applied to the other BET rebodyings of the time, but in practice they were handled together. Tynemouth T100 (FT 4500) is seen ready for delivery with body 2974.

supply was made conditional on export effort, despite the strength of home-market demand. It was hoped that, by gaining a foothold overseas, British companies could establish a continuing flow of export orders that could be expanded once the immediate post-war peak of demand among their domestic customers had been met.

In the immediate post-war period, Bristol had begun to take export orders in this way but at first these had not been linked to ECW bodywork. A batch of special L-type chassis exported to various South African operators had been well received and the Johannesburg dealer involved, Trucks & Transport Equipment, placed a repeat order for 50, this time with ECW bodywork. These were 30ft. long and 8ft. wide, with Gardner 6LW engines, and the chassis

were accordingly designated LWL6G, a form of designation then unfamiliar in Britain (where 27ft. 6in. was still the maximum length for single-deckers and 8ft. width was only permitted in place of the usual 7ft. 6in. for approved routes from 1946, which made it still quite rare).

It was considered that climatic conditions favoured an almost all-metal structure, and thus the bodies of these South African vehicles had aluminium alloy main pillars, waistrails and cant rails, the only wood in their structure being yang packing in the bearers and main pillars and Columbian pine floorboards. Apart from their dimensions and form of construction, they had clear resemblances to the standard home-market design, though a porch-style entrance at the front was incorporated and the windows

The first of the batch of 50 export single-deckers on Bristol LWL6G chassis for South Africa is seen here on tilt test and, below, ready for shipping in May 1948. It had body 2360 and was destined for Greyhound Bus Lines, which had six of the vehicles. The tilt test view shows impressive stability with the test table on 35° and the body showing under 41°. Also evident is the large external oil-bath air cleaner alongside the bonnet. The 8ft. width gave significantly different frontal proportions compared to the standard 7ft. 6in body as built for the Tilling group on L-type chassis, of which one is visible in the background. The three-quarter view shows the well-proportioned lines and the porch-type front entrance, a feature which would doubtless have been preferred by some home-market customers who had to accept the rigid standardisation imposed by Tilling policy; greater indulgence to gain export business was common at the time. The continuous 'louvred louvre' over the windows was a feature commonly found on South African buses of the period. Most of the buses seated 39, though five for Vaal Transport (2373-7) are recorded as seating 46.

were of the half-drop type with deep louvres above. They were supplied during 1948 to eight operators, including the municipalities of Benoni (which took 15 vehicles), Springs (12), Germiston (8) and Roodepoort (2), plus Greyhound Bus Lines (6), Vaal Transport (5), Anglo American Corporation (1) and the Electricity Supply Commission (1). The last of the 50, one of the Benoni vehicles, was exhibited at the 1948 Commercial Motor Show at Earls Court, London, and doubtless when this was arranged there were high hopes of further export business.

That Show, held in September 1948, was the first since the 1939-45 war and all the major British manufacturers were represented. There were three exhibits with ECW bodywork on the Bristol stand – a K6B with highbridge body for the Lincolnshire fleet, an L6B with 31-seat 'express' body for United and the Benoni LWL6G mentioned above. It was perhaps a little surprising that Bristol and ECW were present at the Show at all, in view of the changes to the transport industry that were then taking place.

This view of fourteen of the Bristol LWL6G buses for South Africa lined up in front of the works prior to delivery on 25th August 1948 is thought to include those with body numbers 2384 to 2397, mainly for various municipal fleets though including the single vehicle for the Electricity Supply Commission and a Greyhound example – they were in primer so individual identification is not possible. It was ironic that a promising export trade was snuffed out almost as soon as it had begun by the requirement, inserted in the Transport Act of 1947 as a concession to the Opposition, that the British Transport Commission subsidiaries could manufacture only for BTC concerns. ECW became governed by this following its sale along with other Tilling bus interests in November of that year.

The final vehicle of the batch, with body 2409 for Benoni Municipality, was exhibited at the Commercial Motor Show in November 1948. This view shows the single rear window, horizontally hinged to act as an emergency exit. There was no external cab door, the driver reaching his seat via the passenger saloon. The fleetname was shown in English on the nearside and Afrikaans on the offside, in a similar manner to that adopted in more recent years by several operators in Wales.

When the Red & White group decided to purchase ECW bodywork for 25 double-deckers for delivery in 1948, both concerns were private enterprise businesses, though the Tilling takeover by BTC was being negotiated. Red & White held an Albion agency, and had chosen this make for most of its fleet requirements for many years but the use of ECW bodywork was a new departure. The chassis chosen was the Albion Venturer CX19, with Albion 9-litre oil engine. The bodies (2981-3005, not batched) were of 55-seat lowbridge type, basically very like the standard type, though the Albion bonnet line was quite high; a slight step was also introduced in the cab front profile. Delivery was made in July-August 1948. Eight of the vehicles were for United Welsh and the remainder for Red & White's own fleet, including the vehicle shown, though it was soon transferred to another subsidiary, Cheltenham & District Traction Co, in whose fleet it was photographed in May 1964. In 1950, the Red & White group had also sold out to BTC, and the Cheltenham undertaking was transferred to Bristol Tramways, run as a separate concern with its own livery.

The 1948 programme included no less than 321 lowbridge bodies on Bristol K chassis for Tilling group companies. They were mainly in one long sequence of body numbers, 2479-2791, but also included two small batches, 3452-4 and 3542-6, the total being built in batches 24 to 34, the later ones of which included other vehicles. They were delivered between August 1948 and July 1949, the majority thus dating from after the transfer of the group to State ownership. United BDO105 (LHN 305) a K5G with body 2705 dating from the Spring of 1949, seen here in Scarborough in July 1950, soon after reaching United after spending its first year on loan to London Transport in the manner described in the text, was typical. The design was virtually unchanged from the 1947 pattern, though the two nearside outlets for water draining from the upper deck floor had been introduced shortly before the 1948 programme began. Flush-fitting sidelamps, as also seen here, were introduced from batch 25. The side destination originally fitted had already been panelled over. Also in seen is BDO14, a Bristol GO5G of 1936, again with a 1949 ECW body (3157).

Chapter Two: **State ownership**

The Labour Government elected in July 1945 instigated and followed a policy of nationalisation of the major service industries including transport. The Transport Act 1947 provided for the creation of the British Transport Commission, which took over the four main-line railway companies and London Transport on 1st January 1948. The railway shareholdings in bus companies in England, Scotland and Wales were also transferred, giving the BTC a large stake in most of the major company undertakings in the Tilling, BET and the Scottish Motor Traction groups but not, at that stage, complete control. However, early in 1948 negotiations began with Tilling for the sale of that group's road passenger transport interests to the BTC.

At that time Sir Frederick Heaton – who had expressed the view during the war that some form of unified transport system was desirable – had hoped that Bristol's

manufacturing interests as well as Eastern Coach Works could have been retained by Thomas Tilling Ltd, along with other activities not to be taken over by the BTC. It was no doubt this hope that prompted ECW's participation in the Earls Court Show. When the announcement of the agreement on the sale was announced that same month, however, it was revealed that this had not proved possible – the problem was the fact that at that stage, the Bristol Tramways & Carriage Co Ltd had no separate subsidiary for its chassis manufacturing department; even though Bristol Commercial Vehicles Ltd had been registered in 1943, no transfer of activities to it had been made.

This gave the BTC its own 'in house' manufacturing facilities, but under the terms of the 1947 Act, no BTC subsidiary was allowed to accept orders from any concern outside the Commission for manufactured goods. This

The 1948 programme highbridge bodies incorporated the upper-deck 'waterspouts' on the nearside, plus one on the offside. The aluminium alloy framing extended to the main pillars, waist rails and cant rails on the lower deck, though upper-deck cant rails were mainly Colombian pine, this applying also to the lowbridge version. The highbridge bodies for K-type chassis totalled 131, numbered 2792-2918, and 3776-9, mainly built in batches 35 to 38, each of which comprised 30 bodies, the exceptions being the eleven four-bay vehicles shown in separate illustrations. Delivery began in July 1948, that of standard examples being completed in June 1949. Among the later examples was body 2900, on Eastern Counties LKH137 (HPW 137), one of 38 K5G highbridge buses for that fleet diverted to London Transport for its first period of duty and seen here operating from Putney Bridge garage on route 93 in October 1949 – it was one of the last two to operate in London, leaving on 2nd June 1950.

The photograph shows the way these buses were adapted for temporary London service, in their owning companies' liveries but without fleetnames and carrying a London Transport roundel on the radiator grille. The upper part of the destination blinds carried London Transport lettering and the lower part 'lazy' blinds for the route operated. Brackets for the garage and running number plates were attached to the side panels. By that date the K-type chassis had bonnet sides without louvres, but a more important change was the adoption of flexible engine mountings for Gardner-engined models, introduced towards the end of the period when such buses were being diverted for London duty, greatly reducing the internal noise and vibration level.

clause had been added to the provisions of the Act at Opposition request to prevent what was considered unfair competition with commercial firms. There were also restrictions on the total volume of bus bodybuilding work which could be carried out, even within the BTC empire, though the way these were framed left ECW able to continue its traditional role as supplier to the ex-Tilling operating companies now part of BTC.

There was widespread disappointment among operators remaining outside BTC which had been Bristol or ECW customers, however, including those in the newly-found export markets, now no longer able to place orders. Fortunately work in hand could be completed and some operators had placed long-term contracts which provided for the supply of vehicles over an extended period. It seems possible that one or two of these may have foreseen the possible turn of events and placed orders before the transfer to BTC ownership took effect. The actual sale of the Tilling interest in road passenger transport and associated activities, which of course included ECW, to the BTC took place on 5th November 1948, although technically it was deemed to have been effective from 31st December 1947, thus entitling the Commission to profits made after that date.

It was expected at that time that the individual operating companies would gradually be taken over by area boards, somewhat akin to London Transport in structure, that were proposed by the Government (the first being planned to cover Northumberland, Durham and part of North Yorkshire). A body called the Tilling Association which had been set up some time previously to administer the group's affairs, was retained in the expectation that its function would gradually dissolve away as the new organisation for the industry took shape. In practice, this did not happen and the now State-owned bus companies in England and Wales continued to be referred to as the Tilling group right up to its incorporation in the newly-

formed National Bus Company on 1st January 1969. Thomas Tilling Ltd continued to exist, but with no connection with its former bus interests.

The first BTC ownership of bus undertakings outside the London area had arisen in April 1948 when Midland General Omnibus Co Ltd and related concerns, which had come into State ownership as a consequence of being owned by an electricity supply company newly nationalised, were transferred to the Commission. Early in 1949, the main Scottish operating companies in the group then headed by the Scottish Motor Traction Co Ltd sold out in a similar manner to Tilling, followed in February 1950 by the Red & White group. Operating companies in all of these groups were initially committed to their existing suppliers of both chassis and bodies for new vehicles but subsequently and gradually they began to receive new Bristol and/or ECW products, although in some cases there was a delay of several years. In Scotland the new group headed by Scottish Omnibuses Ltd (later known as the Scottish Bus Group) at first continued to obtain most of its vehicles from other sources, though ECW began to figure among its suppliers from mid-1951, and regular deliveries of new Bristol-ECW vehicles began in December 1954.

The change of ownership caused only a modest change to ECW. Output dropped slightly in 1949 to 843 and again in 1950 to 705, but this was still well above the pre-war level. Inevitably, the proportion of work for other than Tilling fleets dropped but there was still a strong overall demand. Indeed, an almost immediate consequence of the incorporation of the Tilling companies into the British Transport Commission was a decision to divert temporarily new double-deckers being built for these companies to help in overcoming a severe shortage of serviceable buses being experienced by London Transport, by then also a BTC responsibility. The London fleet was suffering serious problems with the bodywork on many of

Single-deck production on new chassis was comparatively modest in the 1948 programme, with 111 Bristol L (2919-69 and 3254-3313), nearly all built at Irthlingborough and not batched. Of these, 108 were 35-seat buses on a mixture of L5G, L6A and L6B chassis, with no significant variations except that body 2948 for Hants & Dorset had half-drop windows. Three were 31-seat express L6B, one (2962) for United acting as one of the exhibits at the 1948 Show and the following two (2963-4) for United Counties – these three had a more modest single-aperture front destination box than previous express bodies and rather reminiscent of a late 'thirties ECW pattern, as shown by United Counties 808 (EBD 235) with body 2964 seen here.

its pre-war buses as a delayed consequence of unavoidable wartime neglect when the normal overhaul facilities were diverted to the construction of bombers, quite apart from the problem of numerous over-age vehicles common to most operators.

The vehicles selected were all Bristol K5G or K6A models with ECW bodywork and the initial diversions comprised 145 lowbridge and 45 highbridge buses drawn from twelve operating companies, though the largest contributors were Crosville (with 43, plus a further six at a later stage), Hants & Dorset (39) and Eastern Counties (38 highbridge). The intention was that each would spend a year in London Transport service before delayed delivery to their rightful owners. The loans began in December 1948 but a further eleven lowbridge buses were diverted in November 1949 to allow some of the early vehicles to be released, the scheme not ending until June 1950. The buses were painted in their standard Tilling green and red livery (apart from seven Brighton Hove & District in Brighton red and cream) bearing the owner's fleet numbers but no fleetname, and were delivered direct from Lowestoft to Chiswick. Other ECW output during this period was delivered direct to the destined operators as usual, including

Bristol K6B double-deckers, not chosen for London use because their engines were not found in the LTE fleet. The lowbridge bodywork fitted to the majority of the loaned buses was completely unfamiliar to most London passengers, for the vehicles were distributed widely among LTE garages and many worked on trunk routes into and across central London, though ten were used to augment a small ageing fleet of lowbridge buses in service in the Country area.

Throughout the period up to 1950, the standard ECW body styles as established in 1946 continued with only minor changes in appearance. The original style of square-cornered top-sliding windows was replaced from 1947 production with the version using rounded top corners, the whole assembly being included in the rubber glazing surround so that the outlines of opening and non-opening windows became uniform along the sides of the vehicle. Other very small changes were made from time to time, and occasionally experimental features would be tried out on single vehicles or small batches, as indicated in some of the illustrations. Quite often Eastern Counties was the recipient of such vehicles, so that an eye could be kept on their behaviour in service.

What were officially called reconditioned Bristol chassis, of contemporary L type but with special R-suffix chassis numbers, received a further 42 saloon bodies in 1949, built at Lowestoft as part of batch 40, United receiving 32 (3355-86) and Eastern Counties ten (3402-11). This was actually an exercise in circumventing restrictions on BTC's manufacturing activities for the chassis were to contemporary design. Some, notably the Eastern Counties buses which were L4G models with Gardner 4LW engines, and 20 of the United batch which were L5G, may have received engines from older withdrawn buses theoretically 'rebuilt', but this could hardly have applied to the twelve United L6B. Eastern Counties LL408 (body 3411) of this type is seen here – the fitting on the front dash is a type of air intake favoured by ECOC at the time. Visible in this view are the wooden top-rail seats standardised for a time.

Rebodying of sound chassis had been common policy in Tilling-controlled companies since the 'thirties, but ECW's involvement had dwindled in the immediate post-war period. However, this changed quite dramatically in the 1948 programme, though deliveries did not get under way until late in that year and most took place in 1949, rather later than the comparable exercise for BET fleets. There were some 139 lowbridge double-deckers alone, but the key feature was the variety of chassis involved, which must have kept the drawing office busy adapting standard designs. Most of the work was batched, and batches 41 and 42, totalling 58 bodies (3074-99, 3153-4/61-78, 3317-26, 3429-30), were built for Crosville, Hants & Dorset, Southern Vectis, United and United Counties, all being 53-seaters on early Leyland Titan chassis. Most were of the TD2 type of 1932-3, but they included twelve of the earlier but dimensionally similar TD1 model (one of a pair of these from the Southern Vectis fleet dated from late 1929 and had thus begun on its 20th year when redelivered in January 1949). The TD1 and TD2 were quite differently proportioned to later models, with the front bulkhead set further back, and thus the same technique as for the PD1 was adopted, though the short length of the first main bay was even more evident. In addition, the driving position was relatively low and on most examples the top of the windscreen was lowered by about 3in, no doubt to allow the windscreen wiper arc to be at a better relationship to the driver's eye level. Many of the vehicles received the special radiator made by Covrad to modernise the appearance of Leylands of that period, the overall effect being quite smart, as shown by Crosville M25 (FM 6919), a TD2 dating from early 1932 with body 3096, seen at Llandudno in June 1951. Like many such vehicles, it had been fitted with an oil engine, in this case a Leyland 8.6-litre unit in 1935/6. The ability to accomodate 'Llandudno Junction' in full in readable form demonstrates the potential of the destnation display.

By comparison, the later types of pre-war Titan were a more straightforward job, the body design being basically as already built for East Kent and Ribble, though seating 55 when built to Tilling specification. Batch 45 covered a TD3 for Crosville (3100) and one TD3, four TD4 and eight TD5 models for Eastern National (3140-52), delivered between May 1949 and February 1950. Seen here with body 3141 is Eastern National 3659 (ENO 937) a 1937 TD4 originally having an Eastern Counties body, as running after 1954 when it was renumbered 1108. By that date, its original Leyland 8.6-litre oil engine and gearbox had been replaced by a Gardner 5LW and Bristol gearbox; it ran in this form until withdrawal in 1964.

Another chassis which raised difficulties, almost literally, was the Bristol GO5G, even though the end result, with PV2 radiator, was quite like a new or rebodied K-type. The G-type chassis was not as low-built as the K or other comparable makes. Its midships-mounted gearbox was relatively deep, and the solution adopted was to mount the basically standard body slightly higher than usual. This meant that the windscreen could have a horizontal bottom edge while still sufficiently above the radiator, though the overall effect created an optical illusion that the radiator was lower than on a K-type chassis. Some 29 lowbridge bodies (3131-9/55-60, 3202-5, 3431-40) were built in batch 44 for Eastern National, United, Westcliff and Southern and Western National between January and August 1949. There appears to have been a slight shortening of the first body bay, but 55 seats were still accomodated. Seen here is Eastern National 3634 (DEV 470), the chassis of which dated from 1936, with body 3138.

The AEC Regent was also a case where previous experience was helpful, even though the chassis of the six vehicles rebodied in 1948 for Crosville (bodies 3101-6, not batched) dated back to 1931-32. They were originally in the Brighton-based fleet of Thomas Tilling Ltd, having been acquired by Crosville in 1945-6. This was another instance where later-type radiator, bonnet and mudguards were fitted, in this case of the Regent II pattern. In addition, AEC 7.7-litre oil engines were fitted in place of the original petrol units and the chassis frames were replaced with the later 16ft 3in wheelbase type, thus allowing a standard-length body seating 55 to be fitted. Seen here is MA605 (GP 6238) with body 3102. Rather surprisingly after so thorough a reconstruction, they were dismantled in 1954, the bodies going to later Bristol K chassis and chassis parts to spares.

Simplest of all the lowbridge rebodyings of the 1948 programme from ECW's viewpoint were the Bristol K5G types (body numbers 3179-99, 3412-20), which were dealt with alongside new chassis in Batches 29-34 during 1949, receiving identical bodywork. Hants & Dorset had nine and West Yorkshire 21, all being early examples of the model dating from 1937-8. Seen here in Leeds is West Yorkshire 357 (BWY 989) as it had been when it received body 3191, though renumbered DG11 when the photograph was taken. Replacement of the tall radiator of pre-1945 K-types by the PV2 version was routine when they were rebodied by ECW.

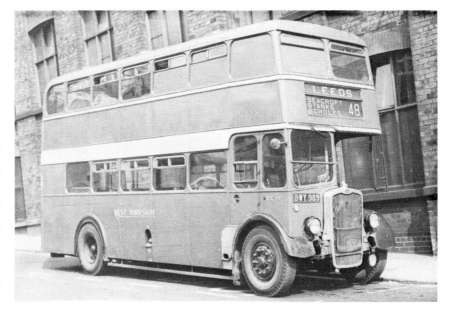

Only one operator in the Tilling group took highbridge bodies as part of the 1948 rebodying programme, this being Bristol Tramways, which sent 48 of its Bristol G-type chassis, which were re-delivered over a nine-month period beginning in November 1948. The chassis were drawn from quite a wide range of the operator's fleet of this type, some having begun life as petrol-engined models dating from 1935-6 while others from 1935-7 had always been GO5G, to which specification all had been converted. Some had begun in the fleet of Maidstone & District but had been exchanged for K5G models early in life. The chassis were fitted with PV2 radiators and the bodies were mounted a couple of inches or so higher than on a K chassis in the same way as used for lowbridge examples. The first 36 (3206-41) seated 56 passengers in the usual way, but the last twelve (3243-53) seated 59, with 28 in the lower deck and 31 above. Bristol 3079 (EAE 288) with chassis dating from 1937 and ECW body 3226 of February 1949 is seen in the livery with cream window surrounds briefly adopted by Bristol for its own fleet in 1951. A further 35 similar 59-seat bodies (3911-45) were built for the Bristol company's fleet of Bristol G-type chassis later in 1949 and January 1950, these being the last to use the combination of framing largely in aluminium but with timber upper-deck cant rails.

Single-deck rebodying also got under way in the 1948 programme, some 115 examples going to various Tilling companies between November of that year and January 1950. United sent 30 Leyland Tiger TS7 models dating from 1935-6, all oil-engined from new, half of which had been Burlingham-bodied coaches originally used on the London-Newcastle services and the others Eastern Counties-bodied buses, for which largely standard 35-seat bodies (3025-57) were built at Irthlingborough, unbatched in the usual way. The body design needed only mild alteration to suit the TS7 chassis, as can be seen from this view of LTO 25 (BHN 275) in the bus station and garage premises jointly occupied by United and what was still generally called SMT (legally Scottish Omnibuses) in Berwick in August 1953.

The Caledonian Omnibus Co Ltd, based in Dumfries, was still the Tilling group's outpost in Scotland when eight single-deckers were selected for rebodying by ECW, the work being done at Lowestoft in batch 43 in February-March 1949. They could hardly have been more complex in terms of modifications to the standard body. Four of them (3123-6) were on Leyland Lion LT2 chassis dating back to 1931, two (3127/8) on Lion LT5 of 1932 and two (3129/30) on Dennis Lancet II of 1938, all having Gardner 5LW engines, the Lancets from new. The LT2 not only had the usual front-end layout of Leylands of the pre-1933 era but had a short wheelbase, so the body structure was shortened in the foremost bay as can be seen by the emergency door in this view of Caledonian 73 (SM 8854). It is seen in Carlisle after it had become Western SMT 854, though still in Tilling red – the Caledonian concern was absorbed by Western in 1950. The seating capacity was 31, but the LT5, with similar front-end and a longer wheelbase allowed 33; Crosville also had one LT5 similarly rebodied (3122), completing the same batch. The Lancet II buses seated 35 as rebodied.

United Counties chose to retain the original tall radiator when having sixteen Bristol JO5G rebodied, and the cab front, with step below the much shallower windscreen than standard, was reminiscent of that on the original Lowestoft-built bodies of 1936-7. The new bodies (3058-73) were built at Irthlingborough in 1949, No. 450 (VV 5696) with body 3072 is preserved, as shown here. It is noteworthy that Bristol, when having 28 JO5G rebodied for its own fleet (3327-54) at about the same time, fitted PV2 radiators. and this also applied to eleven L5G for Hants & Dorset (3314-6 & 3421-8), the latter sharing batch 40 with the new buses on L5G R-suffix chassis which were regarded as 'rehabilitation' jobs to meet the requirements of officialdom. Caledonian took four bodies (4241-4) built in June 1949 as part of batch 65 on 1939/42 L5G chassis in the 1949 programme.

However, the most important alteration in design caused no alteration in external appearance, though it did cause a revision internally. This was the change-over to aluminium alloy as the main material for the body framing, already mentioned in connection with the South African order. The first step in this direction was taken with the use of aluminium alloy pillars in a one-off lowbridge K5G for Eastern Counties – body number 1230, delivered on 2nd July 1947, as LK30 (registered HAH 230). A highbridge body was built later that year with steel front bulkhead, light alloy pillars and other framework, and an internal view was published in an advertisement in the trade press in November 1947.

Previously English oak or ash had been used for the main pillars, with a mixture of woods for waist and cant rails – it was quite common for five different types of timber to be used in various parts of the framing. In many cases, different woods would be used in offside and nearside waist and cant rails of double-deckers. Elm, mahogany, pine and spruce were generally used in the riser boards, whilst yang was used for bulkheads and for the upper-deck pillars of double-deckers. At about the same time, May 1948, as the first of the South African Bristol LWL buses were built, aluminium alloy main pillars were used in 34 lowbridge bodies built on Leyland TD4 and TD5 chassis dating from 1936 to 1938 for East Kent. Their body numbers 2410-2433 followed on from the South African batch 2360-2409.

Use of aluminium alloy for framing was gradually extended and there were many cases of double-deckers with lower-deck cant rails in alloy and upper-deck rails in timber – the last recorded instance of this combination being body 3945, a rebodied Bristol GO5G for the Bristol Tramways fleet, its number 3814, delivered on 30th

Crosville carried out another complex rebuilding exercise with fifteen buses drawn from its J class of Leyland Lion LT7 models of 1935, which originally had Leyland four-cylinder oil engines and Eastern Counties bodies. The chassis were fitted with Leyland 8.6-litre six-cylinder engines, these requiring a longer bonnet than the short original item. The new bodies (3107-21) were almost to standard 35-seat pattern, though the windscreen was more raked to suit the front dash position, flush with the original 'slim' radiator, which was retained. The end result, reclassified JA, was quite attractive, as can be seen from this view of JA23 (FM 8993) with body 3110, in Llandudno in June 1951. These vehicles re-entered service in May 1949 and in September of that year the balance of ten were similarly dealt with, receiving bodies 4245-54 in the 1949 programme, but these were fitted with Gardner 5LW engines, being then reclassified JG.

Included among the 1948-programme rebodyings were five Leyland Tiger TS4 models which had begun life as coaches in 1933 and, perhaps because of this history, in 1949 received 31-seat express bodies 3443-7, as well as 8.6-litre oil engines. Seen here at Llandudno is KA192 (FM 7471) with body 3446. As usual with rebodied Leylands of that generation, they received Covrad 'modernising' radiators. These were built at Lowestoft but one further express body (3441) was also built for Crosville, but at Irthlingborough on a Tiger TS6 chassis.

January 1950. From then on aluminium alloy was the general constructional material, though timber continued to be used for bearers and floorboards, and there was a reversion to yang for the main pillars and waistrails and initially for cant rails, in the various batches of coaches which were built in 1950-51.

The switch from timber to aluminium had a practical benefit in that the body sides were slimmer, giving a small but useful gain in internal width, particularly important while 7ft. 6in. was still the usual overall width, which continued to be so for almost all ECW bodies built up to 1950. The internal appearance of the body sides was rather plain with a slight vertical ridge at each pillar but no other break in the interior panelling other than the glazing rubber for the window itself – the surface had a leathercloth or similar type of finish.

Mention of the near-universality of 7ft. 6in. width in ECW output prior to 1950 draws attention to the only home-market exceptions to this pattern of production. The limited interest in the route-approval procedure required before 8ft. vehicles could be operated in the 1946-50 period tended to be focused on urban areas, among them Middlesbrough where the Corporation transport department chose this width for its post-war ECW bodywork. This town had been a consistent customer for ECW bodywork in 1937-40, when 26 bodies to ECW's standard outline had been supplied on Leyland Titan TD5c and TD7c chassis, representing the fleet's entire intake over that period. Early post-war deliveries to this fleet were from other bodybuilders, but an order was placed with ECW covering two batches of sixteen double-deck bodies before the ban on accepting orders from non-

The 'slim-sided' construction made possible by ECW's choice of aluminium-framed body design is shown by this view of a double-deck body before the seats were installed. The vehicle is one of the experimental four-bay bodies constructed as part of the 1948 programme, this photograph dated 20th July 1949 showing body 2865, the first of the twelve such bodies, completed the following month as Eastern Counties LKH102. The aluminium framing concept was well established by then, experimental bodies having been constructed in 1947. The system was adopted progressively for most production bodies from mid-1948, though upper-deck cantrails did not switch from wood until early in the 1949 programme.

The experimental four-bay highbridge 56-seat bodies built in 1949 were unusual among double-deckers of this form in that the four main body bays stretched the full length of the lower saloon instead of the design incorporating a short bay, usually without window, just ahead of the rear platform, as on the London RT and other comparable designs of the period. The effect was a little strange-looking and this may be why it was not repeated when the production four-bay bodies for Bristol KS-type chassis went into production the following year. All twelve were produced as batch 46 and all but two were in the 1948 programme, though all were delivered between August and October 1949. Eastern Counties was the main recipient, with nine (2865-9 and 2902-5), one went to the York-West Yorkshire fleet (2918), one to Brighton Hove & District (3779, the only one on a K5G, the others all being K6B), and one for Bristol Tramways (3827), these last two being in the 1949 programme. Seen here is Eastern Counties LKH140 (HPW 140) before delivery in August.

The first 16 vehicles in Middlesbrough Corporation's postwar order were included in the 1948 programme, though built between March and October 1949. They were for 8ft.-wide bodies (3006-21) on Leyland PD1/3 chassis and the appearance was almost identical to that of the bodies built for Bristol on PD1A chassis, apart from the extra width and the usual specification details. Number 59 (ADC 659), with body 3012, is seen in service in August 1956 – note Middlesbrough's use of letters rather than numbers for route identification.

The second part of the Middlesbrough order, a further sixteen 8ft. bodies, were quite different, and not only because they were on Guy Arab III chassis with Gardner 6LW engines, reputedly because Leyland was unable to supply chassis by the date required, unusually for that concern. ECW was busy with the second Lodekka prototype, as described in the next chapter and it is significant that the Middlesbrough buses had body numbers 3854-69 immediately following that vehicle. There were several affinities in the design, four-bay to the more usual $4\frac{1}{4}$ pattern, having taller windows and a less rounded outline. The low-mounted Guy radiator gave an effect a little like that of the rebodied GO5G, with quite a deep but fairly narrow windscreen. Number 69 (AXG 669) is seen at the town centre bus station.

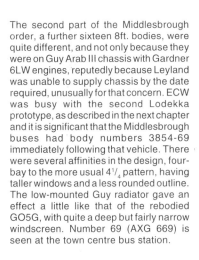

49

This view of a Middlesbrough Guy shows how the '4½-bay' layout gave a longer window at the rear of the upper-deck side panels, with room for a destination display below it without cutting into the line of the pillar in front of it. The lines of the body as a whole were rather upright, unusually so for that period. The vehicle shown is No. 69, with body 3854.

ECW had produced another body (3512) with unusual window outlines the previous autumn. This was a one-off experiment on a Bristol K6B, allocated, as so often the case, to Eastern Counties, as its LK 366 (KNG 366) and delivered in September 1949, included in the 1949 programme of some 320 lowbridge bodies on K chassis (3448-51/5-3541/7-3775) in batches 48 to 58 delivered between September 1949 and July 1950. The tall windows on the nearside were intended to give a better view to standing passengers, the offside being quite standard due to the presence of the upper-deck gangway at the corresponding level. Neither the design nor the livery style, also experimental and soon altered to standard, were pursued, and in general production models followed the previous year's pattern, save that metal-framed double top rail seats had become standard. The nearside indicator over the entrance was omitted after only a handful of bodies built before the end of October 1949 had gone through.

BTC undertakings took effect.

The first batch were on Leyland Titan chassis of the PD1/3 type and the bodywork (ECW numbers 3006-21) built for them was generally similar to that built in 1947 on the equivalent 7ft. 6in. PD1 chassis for the Bristol Tramways fleet, apart from the increased width and the operator's preference in destination display and other minor details. They were delivered between March and September 1949, by which date the PD1 had become quite a rare choice, having been superseded generally by the more powerful PD2.

The second batch for Middlesbrough (3854-69) were on Guy Arab III chassis and were built the following year. This time the body design, in addition to 8ft. width, differed considerably from the ECW standard pattern as it had become known over the previous few years and indeed gave clear signs of fresh designs then about to appear. The basic outline was less rounded, with a more upright profile and shallower roofline than the previous highbridge standard. There were four bays between

bulkheads, a feature that had been tried on twelve otherwise standard highbridge bodies on Bristol K chassis built in 1949; ten belonged to the 1948 programme, of which nine went to Eastern Counties (2865-69 and 2902-5) and one to the York-West Yorkshire fleet (2918), while two in the 1949 programme, for Brighton Hove & District (3779) and Bristol Tramways (3827), were built later in the year. The Middlesbrough design differed by having deeper windows, the effect being especially marked on the lower deck, and also in having a short bay behind the rearmost main side window on the lower deck. The completed Middlesbrough Guy Arabs were delivered between 5th May and 4th September 1950.

Overall in the 1946-50 period, ECW produced 1,936 double-deck bodies of 26ft. by 7ft. 6in. dimensions (of which 1,372 were lowbridge and 564 highbridge) and 1,331 single-deckers of 27ft. 6in. by 7ft. 6in. size (1,222 stage carriage buses and 109 of the 'express' version), against the production programmes planned for the five years. This was a considerable achievement in terms of

Highbridge body production on Bristol K-type chassis followed a similar pattern in the 1949 programme, with 176 bodies (3780-3850 and 4074-8) built from October 1949 to June 1950 in batches 60 to 62, which also included some bodies from the 1950 programme. Here again, the design was generally unchanged, with the omission of the side destination display as the most obvious change. Generally, seating capacity continued as 56, though Bristol Tramways examples seated 59. Seen here is Brighton Hove & District 6418 (EPM 15), a K5G with body 3790, among the last completed. It displays the distinctive appearance given by the special Brighton red and cream livery, and destination box pattern, both of which were governed by an agreement with Brighton Corporation involving the joint operation of local services. When similar but slightly older BH&D buses were being lent to London Transport, it was found that they would accept standard LT blinds, this being due to the ancestry of the Brighton operation, originally a branch of Thomas Tilling which had operated similar buses in both London and Brighton.

standardisation, quite apart from the numbers built. There were also the vehicles to larger dimensions mentioned above and others of an experimental nature described in the next chapter.

Contributing to this total was the Irthlingborough works, which resumed the construction of new bodywork when the urgent demand for repair and rebuild work that had arisen as operators sought to get their fleets back into better condition when the war ended began to tail off. This time the output was entirely of single-deck bodies of identical design to those built at Lowestoft and numbered in the main Series 2 sequence. Nearly all the parts were

fabricated at Lowestoft and transported by road to Irthlingborough for assembly. In practice, it was sometimes possible to identify them by a slight difference in front number plate position.

The first example was a standard 35-seat L5G for United (fleet number BLO 164), body number 1322, delivered on 3rd February 1947. About 100 bodies were produced per year, although it is not possible to be certain of exact numbers as there are some discrepancies in the records. Production continued until May 1952 – further reference to this appears in the next chapter.

Single-deck output on L-type chassis also continued much as before, again with omission of the side destination box, in this case replaced by an opening window. There were 224 standard 35-seat bodies for Tilling companies (3960-4061/7-73, 4095-4194, 4197-4211), of which 142 (including 86 for United) were built at Irthlingborough but these appeared to be indistinguishable from Lowestoft products. In addition, Bristol Tramways took delivery of a second batch of its unique type of two-doorway version seating 33 intended for City routes, of which 20 on L5G chassis (bodies 1416-35) dated from 1947. The 1949 programme included 29 (4212-40) delivered in 1949-50 on a mixture of L5G and L6B chassis. The first one, an L5G numbered C2732 (LHY 972) with body 4212 is seen here before delivery. The additional door at the front was of the same sliding type as at the rear, and was accomodated by a rather awkward division of the first two bays.

Maidstone & District was a BET company which had been a regular Bristol purchaser since 1937 but not with ECW bodywork, though there had been 34 Leyland Tiger TS8 buses so bodied in 1938. The early post-war emphasis had been on K6A double-deckers with Weymann bodies, but orders had been placed for L-type singledeckers with ECW bodies before the cut-off point for non-BTC business. The first to be delivered were a batch of sixteen L6A models with 35-seat bodies 4079-94 delivered in 1949-50, by which date the AEC engine option had become quite rare. The body design was based on the Tilling standard version, though with single front destination box and none at the rear; ironically the side display just deleted on Tilling orders was specified. The dark green and cream livery, with a waistband below the side windows and subtle lining out of mouldings, suited the design well.

The 1949 double-deck rebodying programme for Tilling fleets followed a similar pattern to that of 1948, though the peak of demand had passed. Noteworthy among the bodies built were 26 on Leyland TD2 chassis for Eastern Counties. Twelve were lowbridge (3899-3910) and fourteen highbridge (3946-59), and AH212 (NG 5403) of the latter, delivered in 1950, is seen here in Cambridge in November 1957. The chassis dated from 1933. As was usual for Titans in that fleet, a Gardner 5LW engine had been fitted, and in addition to the Covrad radiator, the examples fitted with new bodies at this period also received Bristol-type front wings, accentuating the unusual profile that emerged. Some of these vehicles were among the last of their generation to remain in public service, lasting into the early 'sixties. There were also 29 lowbridge bodies on TD4 and TD5 chassis divided between Crosville and Cumberland (3870-98) and the highbridge bodies on Bristol G chassis for Bristol Tramways already mentioned.

The express 31-seat body on Bristol L chassis continued in production, the 1949 programme including 21 (4256-70/5-80). Among them were eight for Lincolnshire on L6A chassis, of which the vehicle shown was delivered as 741 (FFW 195) with body 4268 late in 1949, though it had been renumbered 2010 when photographed in 1956. The destination box was of the Clayton type which had been standardised by this fleet in the 'thirties and had returned to favour – it was also a local product, the Clayton Dewandre concern being based in Lincoln.

When this official picture of the first prototype Bristol ECW Lodekka was published in the technical press in October 1949, a month after it had been delivered from Lowestoft, it looked very strange, and indeed its odd proportions came as a shock after the balanced functional elegance of the K and L ranges as then being produced. Yet its basic concept of lowering what amounted to a highbridge body sufficiently to eliminate the hitherto normal internal step up from the rear platform was bound to produce the effect of seat and window levels much lower in relation to the bonnet. The resemblence in outline to the standard highbridge body as being built on conventional chassis at the time is obvious and, to lower the driver's position adequately below the upper saloon floor, the steering column was inclined more, producing a relationship with the front axle and wheels almost having a touch of the early Leyland Titan, as can be seen in comparison with the rebodied TD2 shown on the opposite page.
Bristol had introduced a new style of radiator for new conventional models of which chassis were displayed at the 1948 Show, wider and slightly taller than the PV2 unit, and this looked positively massive in relation to the lowered body level. A '$4\frac{1}{4}$-bay' body style was chosen, but the integration of body and chassis structures dictated the pillar positions, resulting in the slightly longer bay over the rear axle. The vehicle, with body 3852, was numbered LC5000 by Bristol Tramways and received the registration LHY 949 in the same series as the L-type shown on page 51, with which it was almost contemporary.

Chapter Three:
A bus design revolution

The Lodekka prototypes

One of the most important events of 1949 at ECW, and indeed in the long run for the British bus industry as a whole, was the construction of the first Bristol Lodekka. Limitations on overall height of double-deckers had been the subject of difficulty since the early days, particularly when top-covered models appeared in the 'twenties. At about the same time, efforts were being made to lower the build of buses generally, to avoid the need for boarding passengers to climb to the high floor levels required by the straight lorry-type chassis frames then in use.

These trends came together in the NS-type double-deckers built by AEC for the London General Omnibus Company, in which a special design of rear axle allowed what then seemed a dramatic drop in frame height, helping to persuade the authorities to allow top-covered double-deckers in London from 1926. The following year Leyland achieved a similar floor height with a simpler chassis layout in their Titan TD1 model but further reduced overall height by about 1ft., using a sunken gangway on the offside of the upper deck, giving the trade name Lowbridge to this layout, though in later years this effectively became part of the language. Rather similarly

The reason why. This platform view of the first prototype Lodekka shows how passengers could walk inside from the platform without stepping up in the way required on conventional double-deckers of the day. The gangway was almost level throughout its length, and in the early days it was quite common to find passengers still making the instinctive move to step up at this point, only for their feet to land with a crash! The original form of rear axle required two massive covers, one on each side of the gangway as seen here – later development greatly reduced the intrusion at this point.

Leyland's Hy-bridge name for a version of conventional layout became 'highbridge'.

The reduced height was of particular value because of the restricted headroom under numerous railway or canal bridges in some parts of the country, many of which were too low to allow taller double-deckers through but would accept the lowbridge type. In some cases the height of garage entrances also dictated the need for lowbridge double-deckers.

Even so, the layout had serious disadvantages – the sunken gangway severely reduced headroom over the offside lower-deck seats, causing many a bumped head on rising, while upstairs the seating, usually four-abreast, was particularly uncomfortable for the passenger seated nearest the gangway if the other three occupants were of broad build and wearing heavy winter overcoats. Access to and from the seats remote from the gangway, again with low headroom, was difficult and fare collection inconvenient for the conductor. Many operators avoided the use of lowbridge buses altogether or confined them to where they were essential. Others, however, particularly in the Tilling group, tended to assign them to all double-

deck routes, mainly for reasons of standardisation or to avoid the risk of accidents caused by a highbridge bus striking a bridge when used on an unsuitable route. In the 1946-50 period, the Tilling group was by far the largest purchaser, with ECW the bodybuilder producing the largest number of such buses, accounting for half the firm's output in the peak year, 1948.

The Lodekka was the result of far closer co-operation than the mere placing of a new design of ECW body on a redesigned Bristol chassis, and was the first instance of a whole series of joint design exercises involving various types of vehicle. The chassis took the principle of the drop-centre rear axle, which had been used in a tentative way on the NS, to its logical conclusion. Another important feature was the elimination of the hitherto conventional body underframe, the lower saloon floor being laid directly on the chassis, and the side pillars of the body attached directly to outriggers forming part of the chassis frame. This latter idea had been used in some London trolleybus designs in the late 'thirties but the Lodekka was the first comparable vehicle to exploit the reduction of height it made possible. The same 1ft. reduction in height as the lowbridge bus gave over the conventional highbridge was achieved, but with normal centre gangways on both decks and full internal headroom throughout their length.

Contemporary accounts indicate that design work began at the Bristol company's Brislington motor construction works (sometimes rather confusingly known by the initials MCW, but having no connection with the bodybuilding firm Metropolitan-Cammell Weymann Ltd more usually identified by those initials) in October 1948, shortly after sale of the Tilling group to the BTC had been agreed. The low floor level and consequent low overall height of the complete vehicle was made possible by the transmission layout of the chassis. The engine in the prototypes, (a Bristol AVW similar to that used in the K6B) was mounted at a conventional level over the front axle but the output shaft of the gearbox mounted behind it emerged at a low level, offset to the right, and a rather complex propeller shaft layout took the drive to an enclosed cross-shaft part-way along the chassis and thence by separate propeller shafts to final drive units, one at each side of the rear axle. Later in the course of development of the prototypes this was simplified, with the low-level cross-shaft incorporated within the rear axle, which thus became of the drop-centre type as also used on later Bristol double-deckers as well as widely copied elsewhere.

As a result, the lower-saloon gangway was at the level of the rear platform, the previous usual step up at the rear bulkhead being eliminated. The gangway was slightly sunken below the general lower saloon floor level, but the remainder of the body had the proportions of a normal highbridge double-decker. A diagram issued when the first prototype was shown to the technical press showed its overall height when laden to be 13ft. 2in., exactly the same as a Bristol K-type chassis with standard lowbridge ECW body, the figure for the ECW highbridge body on a K-type chassis being 14ft. 2in. Unladen height on the Lodekka rose by 2in. – both types of the K rose by $1^3/_4$in.

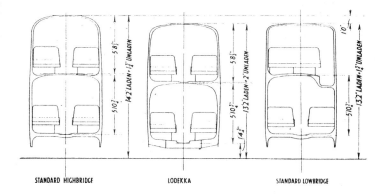

These cross-sections show how the prototype Lodekka combined the internal layout of the highbridge bus with the overall height of the lowbridge type, in both cases using standard ECW bodywork on conventional chassis, doubtless the K-type.

STANDARD HIGHBRIDGE   LODEKKA   STANDARD LOWBRIDGE

The first Lodekka was originally given the chassis number PT149 in what was evidently a prototype series but was renumbered to LDX.001 by the time it had received ECW body number 3852 and been delivered back to the Bristol Tramways company as fleet number LC5000 on 10th September 1949. The 58-seat body design was derived from ECW's standard highbridge body as then in production, with similar roof contour and profile, though having four main bays of which the rearmost was wider than the other three, so as to tie in with the chassis outriggers ahead of and behind the rear axle. The overall length was the then maximum of 26ft. and the width 7ft. 6in. It weighed 7 tons 9cwt unladen.

The overall proportions of the new bus seemed very strange, however, partly because the low waistline made the radiator and bonnet seem more obtrusive. This effect was emphasised because the radiator was much wider than the PV2 type used on the contemporary K – it also appeared to be taller, though this was at least partly due to the low build of the body. It is thought that the radiators and possibly other chassis parts of two prototype chassis of normal height that had been exhibited at the 1948 Show designated the M-type (an MD6G double-decker and

MD6B single-decker) were used for this initial Lodekka and a second similar chassis. It is understood that at least one of the M-type chassis was used for Lodekka development, and it seems clear that the decision not to proceed with the former was related to the latter.

The second Lodekka, LDX.002, was completed in spring 1950 for the West Yorkshire Road Car Co Ltd, becoming number 822. The body, 3853, though of similar layout, had deeper windows on both decks and a general affinity to the Middlesbrough Guy Arab buses being bodied at about the same time. It is shown in ECW records as being delivered on 3rd April 1950, but it is believed to have gone to Bristol initially, passing to Brighton Hove & District in April and not arriving at West Yorkshire's headquarters in Harrogate until 9th June. Both vehicles visited various Tilling companies, spending spells in service under varying operating conditions, and LDX.002 was displayed at the Festival of Britain on the South Bank site in London in August and September 1951. More development and redesign was done before further Lodekka buses were built, but the foundation for the model's success and influence had been laid.

The vehicle looked just as strange from a three-quarter offside view – 'all mouth' might sum up the effect.

55

This comparison of the three-quarter rear views of the first and second Lodekka prototypes emphasises the effect of the revised body design, with its taller windows and the adoption of standard Tilling livery on the second vehicle, West Yorkshire 822 (JWT 712), which had body number 3853, and was completed in the Spring of 1950. The lower saloon waist remained noticeably lower than on a conventional double-decker of the period, only just above the top of the front mudguard, and indeed the appearance of the cab side was to engage ECW designers' attention on subsequent Lodekka types.

Both Lodekka prototypes made a series of visits to associated companies within the British Transport Commission empire. Here the second vehicle, West Yorkshire 822, is seen in Mansfield Woodhouse, operating for Mansfield District Traction Co, in March 1951. The comparison with a 1948 AEC Regent III with Weymann body, No.150 (JVO 946) of that company, is striking. The perspective does not do justice to the difference in height, the AEC being a highbridge bus and about 1ft taller, but the different proportions are very evident – both vehicles were 26ft long and 7ft 6in wide. At that date, the Mansfield company and its associated concerns in the area, which had been members of the Balfour Beatty group prior to becoming State-owned in 1948, had fleets which standardised largely on AEC and Leyland chassis with Weymann bodywork but they were to become Bristol and ECW users within a few years.

Single-deckers without chassis

The first Lodekka was given extensive press coverage, but ECW's first venture in constructing vehicles without chassis entered service without publicity. This may have been because they had been overtaken by a larger-scale venture then being developed, and in one sense they were part of a line of development which had begun elsewhere. The bodybuilding concern John C. Beadle Ltd, of Dartford, Kent had developed a very light form of integral vehicle,

The ECW chassisless buses built for Eastern Counties in 1950 were an interesting exercise that might have had quite a promising future had Bristol and ECW not been involved in the quite different 'Light Saloon' project by the time they were being produced. The choice of half-cab layout for an integral bus was very unusual, suggesting that the Beadle full-fronted vehicles which were their predecessors had been found unsatisfactory in terms of engine access and possibly driver vision. The front-end detailing was quite stylish, with a touch of London RT about the nearside wing treatment and built-in headlamps in line with the latest car practice, even if the radiator was perhaps less inspired. The bonnet was relatively long in relation to the compact Gardner 4LK engine. At the rear, the 'three-window' effect was unique on an ECW body of that period, giving a hint of the RE bus of a dozen years later. Seen above right is CD843 (HPW 828) with 'chassis' number CD12 and body 3398, together with the offside of CD844 and the rear of CD834.

constructing a series of prototypes for various Tilling group companies, using engines, axles and other mechanical units from various existing small buses in the 20-26 seat class. The resulting 'new' vehicles were larger and generally seated 35 and were of full-fronted forward-control layout. Some were also built incorporating new Bedford units as used in the OB model and altogether over 80 had been placed in service by 1949.

It was decided that year that ECW would produce some vehicles of somewhat similar character, though the body appearance, with half-cab layout, was nearer to

ECW's usual standard. A total of 20 Dennis Ace buses with ECW 20-seat bodywork and, unusually for that model, Gardner 4LK engines had been placed in service by Eastern Counties between 1938 and 1940 (see page 108 of my earlier book published by TPC). The engines and other mechanical units from most of these provided a pool from which fifteen sets were provided for the otherwise new ECW chassisless vehicles, as they were called. The general layout and outline was not unlike that of the Tilling standard single-deck body, with rear entrance, though the emergency door was also in the rear bulkhead, making a rare combination – seating was provided for 32 passengers. At the front the mudguard outlines were neatly merged into the body contours but a conventional bonnet and radiator were used, though the latter was of unique outline. It was intended that Eastern Counties would receive all fifteen, given the chassis numbers CD1 to CD15 and body numbers 3387-3401, and these were delivered from April 1950, but in the event one more, CD16 with body 3442, originally intended for United Counties was also delivered to Eastern Counties when completed in the November. Even before the first of these buses were built, ECW and Bristol were involved in a

much larger-scale exercise involving a single-decker of integrated design, described later in this chapter.

Increased dimensions

For years, operators had been pressing for an increase in the maximum permitted dimensions for buses and coaches. It was known by the latter part of 1949 that a slight increase in maximum length for two-axle double-deckers from 26ft. to 27ft. was likely to be granted, but an announcement early in 1950 that the corresponding figure for single-deckers was to go up from 27ft. 6in. to 30ft. came as a surprise, as the Government had previously resisted such a change. These revisions came into effect on 1st June 1950 and in addition a change was made almost immediately afterward which made 8ft. the general width limit for operation throughout Britain in place of the previous 7ft. 6in. – there had been some doubt as to whether the previous route approval system might be retained in some cases, notably for vehicles operating into London.

Manufacturers introduced new or modified models to take advantage of the new dimensions but the period of several months of uncertainty meant that vehicles of old and new dimensions or indeed a mixture of the two were being produced for a while. In addition, some operators, for reasons of standardisation or local route conditions, continued to favour the earlier limits, this applying particularly to width in certain cases. Eastern Coach Works was considerably affected in this way and the company's output in 1950-52 became quite complex in the variety of sizes being built.

Although the new Lodekka and a new single-decker being developed were clearly set to replace the Bristol K and L models, they were not yet ready for production, so revised versions of the latter were produced and were to remain the main types produced by both Bristol and ECW

during the following year or two – indeed somewhat longer in regard to double-deckers.

The 27ft.-long version of the K was designated KS, or KSW if 8ft. wide. The extra 1ft. of length was split between additional body space and a lengthened bonnet and cab assembly, as compared to previous standard K-types, the rear dash being moved rearwards by 6in. to the positon previously used only with the Gardner 6LW engine. This enabled that engine to be specified in conjunction with the new standard ECW body for the KS or KSW chassis, an option which was taken up by several Tilling companies, although not until 1952. The new body was of four-bay type, with a short 'blank' panel at window level just in front of the platform on the lower deck. At the front there was now a slight step in the profile just below the windscreen, this being radiused at the outer edge. The highbridge version received deeper windows and a shallower roof line akin to those seen on the Middlesbrough Guy Arab buses. Seating capacity remained at 55 for the lowbridge version, the extra length being used to improve legroom, but the standard highbridge version now seated 60, with 32 upstairs and 28 down.

The single-deck body was simply lengthened by the insertion of a short extra bay just in front of the rear door, this allowing the seating capacity to be increased from 35 to 39 by virtue of an extra row of seats. In this case there was no change to the design of the front end of the body, the dimension from front of chassis to the bulkhead remaining at 4ft. 6in., as on earlier models, the Gardner 6LW engine still not being available with the Tilling standard single-deck bus body (though it continued to be available as a chassis option for use with other bodywork).

The first examples of these various new types began to appear in the latter half of 1950. On 28th July the first 'long' single-deckers were delivered, all being on LL5G chassis – three built at Irthlingborough (United BG452-4

The first of the 27ft-long lowbridge bodies on the new Bristol KS-type chassis were 30 examples in batch 72, following on immediately from the last new K types at the end of August 1950. Western National 1828 (LTA 938), a KS5G with body 4345, was one of the earliest of these. The 6in extra length of the KS bonnet was added at the rear, causing the bulkhead to move rearwards, and the wheelbase was increased from the 16ft 3in of the K to 16ft 8in. The body, as well as being altered to suit these dimensions, was quite extensively redesigned, even though the characteristic 'ECW look' was still unmistakeable. A '4¼-bay' layout was adopted, and at the front a slightly more rounded outline was adopted, with a three-aperture destination display having a separate three-track number section. The familiar recessing at the top of the windscreen was abandoned and, instead, a slight step was introduced below it, and the screen frame was now angled in plan view to align with the curvature of the upper deck. The lower edges of both windscreen and the bulkhead windows were now curved. Batches 73 and 74 continued further output of KS-type bodies with 7ft 6in width until January 1951, the total reaching 106.

This view of Eastern Counties LK285 (LNG 285), again a KS5G, with body 4290 which was also among the very early deliveries, allows a direct comparison with the contemporary K shown on the opposite page. The very short bay at the rear of the lower deck was panelled rather than glazed, on both sides of the body, though in later years the nearside one was glazed.

The effect of the change in overall width from 7ft 6in to 8ft on the standard lowbridge body is conveyed by this view of two Thames Valley vehicles at Victoria Coach Station. On the right is 595 (FMO 277), a KS6B delivered in January 1951 with body 4376, built in batch 74, while on the left is 638 (GJB 276), a KSW6B delivered in October of that year with body 5078 in batch 93 (1951 programme). Both vehicles were fitted with seating to coach standard and platform doors, refinements introduced that year by Thames Valley for its London-Reading Service B. This service had previously been operated by lowbridge buses of standard specification apart from being fitted with five-speed overdrive gearboxes; 638 was the first example.

with body numbers 4751-3) and two from Lowestoft (United Counties 821 with body 4804 and West Yorkshire 273, almost immediately renumbered 402, with body 4813). The first 27ft. double-deckers, both lowbridge, followed on 25th August – Thames Valley 586, a KS6B (4367) and Westcliff DJN 554 (4409).

The first 8ft. bodies to the new lengths did not leave ECW until December 1950 – Thames Valley 601 (4382), a KSW6B lowbridge, on the 15th and Eastern Counties LL728 (4666), an 8ft. body on a 7ft. 6in. LL5G chassis (a further interim type of variation that was not uncommon for a time) on the 22nd.

Apart from the Middlesbrough double-deckers already mentioned, work for non-British Transport Commission operators faded quite rapidly after the end of 1948, though Maidstone & District had a batch of sixteen Bristol L6A buses in 1949-50 and a final one of fifteen 30ft.-long 39-seat buses (4863-77) on LL5G chassis, apart from one vehicle which was an LL6A. This was the only example of the AEC 7.7-litre engine (by then dropped as a generally available option by Bristol) in a 30ft. L-type chassis. The batch as a whole was remarkable in that although ordered in 1948 they were completed to a specification not then available.

The highbridge version of the 27ft double-deck body incorporated the same alterations in detail design as the lowbridge, but in addition, adopted much the same rather more upright look, with deeper windows and a shallower roof contour, as the Middlesbrough Guy Arab bodies and the second Lodekka prototype. All but nine of the 1950 programme total of 91 highbridge bodies (4447-4537) were of this general type, the exceptions being nine K6B for United (4523-31) which were tacked on to the end of batch 62. The longer versions were built as batches 77, which consisted of 35 bodies to 7ft. 6in. width on KS chassis, built in the latter part of 1950; 78, which covered 33 bodies of 8ft width mainly on KSW chassis, and 79, comprising 14 KSW, these latter two batches largely built around the turn of the year. Brighton Hove & District took eleven 8ft bodied buses, of which four, including 6424 (FNJ 106) with body 4452, were on 7ft 6in wide KS5G chassis – note the deep shadows under the mudguards. It had become number 424 by the time this photograph was taken in August 1961.

The last highbridge bodies of the five-bay design, substantially as built since 1946, were on reconditioned chassis – a final ten 59-seaters on G-type chassis for Bristol (4538-47) completed in the latter part of 1950, and eleven with the usual 56-seat capacity for the York-West Yorkshire fleet in 1951. The latter were built on 1938 K5G chassis that had been very thoroughly rebuilt and updated by the operator, and the end result was only distinguishable from new by the early-type rear axle, as can be judged in this view of Y377 (CWX 665), renumbered YDG64 when seen in the mid 'fifties. It had body 4556.

The 1950 single-deck programme was similarly mixed in dimensions. Bodies 4559-4955 were all on Bristol L, LL or LWL types, but some were built as coaches of the types described in succeeding pages and in the event the Tilling group took 4559-625, 4647-862, 4900-2 and 4952-5 as buses and 4878-87 as express-type bodies, making a total of 301. There were 40 buses of the 35-seat type in batch 80 (ten of which were built at Irthlingborough), to which can be added the express bodies of the same length, which were another instance of the last of their type. They were built on L6B chassis for Crosville and were unbatched. They differed from most of the type in having 35-seat capacity. The example seen was built as KW173 but had been renumbered ELB173 when photographed.

The LL-type 19ft-wheelbase chassis was the basis for 187 bodies of the 30ft.-long 39-seat rear-entrance type in the 1950 programme, built in batches 81 to 83, each of 45 bodies and batches 85 and 86, each of 26 and built at Irthlingborough for United. A typical example is Crosville KW187 (LFM 768), an LL6B with body 4596 built in batch 82 in the autumn of 1950, seen in Llandudno the following June. An additional short bay was inserted into the previous design, immediately behind the rear axle, allowing space for an additional row of seats but giving a slightly untidy effect, particularly on the offside, as seen here. In other respects the design was not revised in the way that applied to the corresponding double-deckers. It is understood that some L-type chassis were recalled from ECW for extension to 30ft, though those actually being bodied were completed at 27ft 6in.

The 30ft-long version of the L-type body still ranked as an elegant bus, as conveyed in this posed view of West Yorkshire 434 (JYG 728), an example of the 8ft-wide version on the Bristol LWL chassis with body 4842, built in batch 84. The added bay was less intrusive on the nearside because of the entrance door, and the overall proportions remained well balanced. This photograph gives visual confirmation that this vehicle began life as an LWL6B, with Bristol AVW engine, the high level access hole at the front of the bonnet side revealing the swing-over oil filler, similar in appearance and action to the radiator cap, used on this engine. In the following year this bus and 430, 433 and 435 of the same batch received Gardner 5LW engines – West Yorkshire took many new buses with the AVW that year and later, so this may have been more of a case of balancing engine stocks than dissatisfaction. The white steering wheel was used to remind drivers that the vehicle was 8ft. wide, then a new feature to that fleet – this was quite common practice at the time. The rear window was divided on the 8ft-wide version.

Maidstone & District's second batch of vehicles ordered from Bristol and ECW before the cut-off for non-BTC business were of a variant not offered or even legal for service in Britain at that date, comprising fifteen 30ft-long 39-seat bodies (4863-77, not batched) on Bristol LL chassis delivered in the last three months of 1950. Most, like SO54 (MKN 203) with body 4865 shown here, were LL5G but one, SO52, was the only LL6A and the last Bristol with an AEC 7.7-litre engine. The body was basically as built for Tilling companies, though with specification similar to the earlier 27ft 6in batch, including the side destination box, fitted in place of the sliding vent over the last full-length window on the nearside.

As with the 27ft double-deckers, there were instances of 8ft single-deck bodywork on 7ft 6in chassis. Of the total of 47 of the wider 30ft-long bodies in batch 84, seven were on 7ft 6in LL chassis, including three on LL5G chassis for Eastern Counties delivered at the end of its 1950-programme single-deck order, in April-May 1951. Seen here some years later is LL731 (LNG 731), by which date the front destination box had been modified by the operator. There was a further instance of LL5G chassis with 'LWL style' bodywork in batch 87, built for Crosville at Irthlingborough in February-April 1951, where eleven of the seventeen were of this type and the remaining six were on LWL5G.

'Real' coaches

Yet another new body design, making a big departure from ECW practice since the war, was the curved-waist full-fronted coach which appeared in the summer of 1950. In the earlier post-war years the Tilling companies had either accepted the 31-seat express version of the standard ECW single-deck body or had coach bodywork more in keeping with the trends of the time built by other concerns such as Beadle, Duple or Harrington on Bristol chassis, usually the L6B though in some cases L6A or L6G. From 1950, however, ECW began to build bodywork suitable for long-distance or touring duties once more, as had been done on a limited scale up to 1939. The curved waistline was widely favoured and by 1950 the full-fronted cab previously quite rare, became more common, partly due to the growth of interest in the new underfloor-engined models beginning to go into production and a consequent decision that front-engined models should not look dated.

ECW's design was in keeping with both these trends, the swept waist treatment being matched by windscreen panels whose outlines curved quite sharply on their lower edges. Constructionally, there was a reversion to earlier practice in that timber – in particular yang (a second quality Burma teak) was used for main pillars, waistrails and, in most cases, cant rails. On the initial version, built to 27ft. 6in. by 7ft. 6in. dimensions on Bristol L6B chassis, the standard PV2 radiator was retained, its curves blending well with the body design. A front entrance layout – by then in general favour for coaches – was incorporated and the standard seating capacity was 31. A standardised cream livery was adopted, with either green or maroon relief to tone with the operating company's standard livery. However, extensive use of polished aluminium trim meant that the secondary colour was confined to the mudguards and a thin strip along the skirt edging. Of this initial design, 38 were built, with Eastern National and United as the largest recipients, taking ten each. United Counties and West Yorkshire each took six, and three each went to Bristol Tramways and Westcliff.

The ECW coach design introduced in May 1950 made a complete break with the idea of a bus-related vehicle, and also, with its full-fronted cab, made a move to counter the danger of being made to seem out of date by the appearance of underfloor-engined models, then just beginning to be regarded as the coming trend. Yet in some ways, it was a reversion to older practice, for ECW had built curved-waistrail bodies with not-dissimilar lines in 1936-39, even if of the half-canopy style then in widespread favour. A further point of reversion to earlier practice was in the construction, basically timber-framed in the manner which had begun to be abandoned by ECW for bus bodywork about two years previously. All 38 bodies built to this original 27ft 6in by 7ft 6in design were based on Bristol L6B chassis, built in batch 69 and delivered between May and November 1950. The body numbers were split up among other body types on L-series chassis in the 1950 programme (4062-6, 4195/6, 4271-4, 4905-7/15-29/37-45). The styling was among the most appealing in the idiom of that period, and the retention of the Bristol PV2 radiator, attractively proportioned in itself and with its curves echoed in those of the bodywork, was effective in giving a similar type of appeal as the more expensive cars of the period. This photograph of United BLO515 (NHN 115), with body 4925, seen in Scarborough Valley Bridge bus station in July 1950, captures not only the appearance of the model, virtually brand new and having the 'crispness' Bristol vehicles of that period had in their first few months, when the front wheel nuts were still clean, but also the atmosphere of holiday travel by coach in that period.

This view of another of United's batch of L6B coaches supplied in the early summer of 1950, with body 4924, shows the rear styling, with curved glass rear windows. The panels over the side windows were illuminated and used by United to advertise its tour and related activities – examples of the type for other fleets did not have this feature.

As with the output of bus bodies, the new maximum dimensions had their impact on coach production. A 30ft. by 8ft. version of the new design was introduced, the additional length being achieved by increasing the length of the window bays. At the front, a major change in appearance was made by concealing the radiator, the panelling being shaped to allow this and introducing a slightly bulbous profile in place of the previous smooth curve. A decorative grille with an elliptical outline which extended beyond the headlamps removed all trace of the chassis identity save for a small plaque on the radiator filler cover. The first 20 of these coaches formed part of

The 30ft by 8ft version of the curved-waist coach body was modified in frontal styling, with the radiator concealed behind a decorative grille. As it happened, although the first examples of this type were included in the 1950 programme, none were completed until January 1951. This photograph, dated 11th of that month, shows Bristol Tramways 2801 (NAE 4) with body 4908, evidently the first to be completed and, like other early examples, on LL6B chassis, of 7ft. 6in. width rather than the LWL6B for which the body was designed. The pattern of body numbers was particularly involved and the production sequence is more easily followed by reference to the batches. The first of the type was batch 70, of 20 bodies, of which the vehicle shown was the first, delivered in the first three months of 1951. They were followed by batches 88 to 91, each of 31 bodies, of which delivery continued through to September; 46 were in the 1950 programme and 78 in the 1951 one. Most of these were LWL6B, with a few more LL6B, but each year's programme also included one instance of rebodying, as illustrated opposite.

The general design of the enlarged version of the coach as introduced at the beginning of 1951 was very similar to the 1950 version apart from the frontal appearance, the extra length and width being achieved by extending the dimensions in a proportionate way. They did look noticeably larger and it was no doubt this that gave rise to the nickname 'Queen Mary', referring to the famous liner which was still apt to be taken as the last word in size. Another, less flattering, name used in some fleets was 'Banana Boat', the analogy here being related to shape, the 1951 version's grille adding to the effect. Southern Vectis 301 (HDL 183), with 37-seat body 4988, was one of the later vehicles in the 1950 programme, built in batch 90 and delivered in June 1951, being seen here in Ventnor the following April.

the same programme as the shorter vehicles and a further 46 were also ordered in 1950, but in effect they became the '1951 model', none entering service before the beginning of the new year.

This longer version of the coach body generally had 35 seats, giving quite generous leg room, though some were 37-seaters. It was designed for the Bristol LWL6B chassis though a few early deliveries were on the LL6B. Larger numbers followed later in 1951 and a few in 1952, bringing the total on Bristol chassis to 163.

There were also some instances of rebodying using essentially the same design. Possibly the most interesting was a 1947 Leyland Tiger PS1 chassis which had entered service in the fleet of South Midland Motor Services, with a 1935 Eastern Counties body, (originally on a rebodied North Western Road Car Tilling Stevens chassis), subsequently transferring to Newbury & District, an associated company, in January 1950. Following the sale of both concerns to the Tilling group. the old body was removed and the chassis lengthened in Thames Vallley's workshops before rebodying by ECW (5464) to what was basically the standard 30ft. by 8ft. coach style but with radiator exposed, being delivered on 6th June 1951, and re-entering service with Newbury & District.

(Above left) Although the curved-waist coach design was very much associated with Bristol L-series chassis, there were exceptions. Two instances of rebodying occurred in 1951, both having unusual features. The Leyland PS1 shown above left had entered service with South Midland in 1947 with a second-hand body and in the aftermath of the take-over of the Red & White group, the chassis was rebuilt to suit 30ft. bodywork by Thames Valley on behalf of Newbury & District, which was to operate it. The chassis was then sent to ECW to receive the 37-seat body shown under the 1950 programme allocations, though as such the number it received was unusually high at 5464. It was built in batch 88 and delivered in June 1951. Its design was basically to 1951 30ft by 8ft. standard, but was unique among such bodies in retaining the exposed radiator frontal appearance, with details much as the 1950 version. It may have been because of the dimensions of the Leyland radiator, and its offset filler cap, that it was decided not to incorporate the new grille. In later years, running for Thames Valley, it was modified slightly, the decorative strips each side of the radiator being removed and a front bumper added.

(Above) The London-based Tilling coach fleet retained an affinity for AEC chassis which could be traced back to the days when Tilling ran AEC buses in London under an agreement with LGOC before the formation of London Transport. As well as taking new AEC coaches, as described in the next chapter, a series of rebuilds of pre-war Regal chassis was undertaken, and the first of these received a 37-seat body in the 1951 ECW programme, numbered 5485 but included in batch 89 and delivered in April 1951, slightly earlier than the Newbury PS1. It was given a new registration number, LYM 727, not as common a practice in those days as more recently, and both this and the body number were adjacent to those of the new Regal IV coaches.

ECW bodywork had not found customers in Scotland beyond the small number of examples sold to Caledonian, based a few miles over the border in Dumfries, until 1951, when in the aftermath of the sale of the SMT group's bus interests to the BTC orders began to arrive from what were now Scottish Bus Group companies. The first on new chassis were thirteen Daimler CVD6 coaches for W. Alexander & Sons Ltd, which had included some earlier 27ft. 6in. long examples of this model with its Daimler diesel engine and preselective gearbox as part of its decidedly mixed post-war fleet additions. The ECW 37-seat coach body was to the 1951 specification, 30ft. by 8ft., and very similar to those on Bristol chassis except that the front panel was modified to suit the rather taller CVD6 bonnet line. They had body numbers 5681-93 and entered service in June 1951. Seen here is D47 (DMS 560) with body 5692).

Also delivered to Scottish Bus group companies around the same time were a total of 21 unbatched new double-deck bodies for Guy and Daimler wartime chassis, a course of action not pursued within the Tilling group. W. Alexander & Sons Ltd ordered six 53-seat lowbridge (5675-80) for Guy Arab chassis, though five of them were for its subsidiary David Lawson Ltd of Kirkintilloch, which in effect formed a sub-section of Alexander, with common fleet numbering. Among the oldest chassis was RO438 (WG 9818),of the original wartime Arab I model, with Gardner 5LW engine, placed in service in October 1942 and redelivered after receiving body 5678 in June 1951. The five-bay body design had a general resemblance to the pre-1950 standard, but with some contemporary features, like the style of windscreen.

Western SMT had the balance of fifteen bodies, of which nine were 53-seat lowbridge (5773-81), three of them for Daimler CWA6 chassis, forming a unique combination, including KR210 (ASD 351) with body 5779, seen below left – the chassis dated from late 1943. The remainder were on Guy Arab chassis, some of them Arab II models, including GY718 (VS 4349), which received body 5777 and had begun life in 1945 with Greenock Motor Services Ltd, a Western SMT subsidiary. In an attempt to disguise this model's protruding radiator, ECW fitted a cab front panel giving a much greater step in the profile than found on other contemporary chassis. Western's remaining six bodies (5660-5), all on Guy chassis, were 56-seat highbridge of similar general design.

Rebodying for Tilling companies had reduced in scale from the 1949-50 period, and only one batch of double-deckers was produced in the 1951 programme, the work being done in 1951-2. This consisted of thirteen 8ft-wide lowbridge bodies ordered by Eastern National for Bristol K5G chassis, including some early examples dating back to 1937-42 and also one chassis, basically dating from 1948, which had been rebuilt on a new frame after an accident and re-registered. All received PV2 radiators and the bodywork, though largely to the five-bay pattern usual for the K chassis including the recessed layout at the top of the windscreen, had the curved shape for the bulkhead window and windscreen lower edges as well as the three-aperture destination box layout at front and rear of the KS type of body. The Eastern National services in the Luton and Bedford areas were transferred to United Counties on 1st May 1952, and FPU 511, originally Eastern National 373, became United Counties 612 as shown – it is seen here in Bedford in May 1959.

To provide a basis for comparison, standard 1951 ECW double-deck body design practice is represented by this example, even though itself unusual in being one of only two batches in that year's programme which were 7ft 6in bodies on Bristol KS chassis. Southern Vectis, covering the Isle of Wight, was one of a number of operators which found the 8ft width a little too much for routes with narrow or twisty roads, and opted for the narrower version for a while. In this case, there were ten lowbridge bodies (5001-10) on KS5G chassis, of which No.756 (HDL 270) with body 5008 is seen here. The other place with similar problems was York where ten highbridge bodies (5165-72 and 5556/7) were supplied on KS6B. The 1951 programme for bodies on KSW-type chassis included 175 lowbridge 55-seat built in batches 92-96 and 107, together with 135 highbridge 60-seat in batches 97-100 and 114.

The 'headquarters' coach fleet of Thomas Tilling Ltd in London, by then re-named Tilling Transport (BTC) Ltd, began a rebuild programme with pre-war AEC Regal chassis purchased from Bristol Tramways, one of which received an ECW coach body (5485) in the 1951 programme, followed by six more (6281-6) in 1952, which differed in being 7ft. 6in. wide and in other details.

More significant in its wider implications was the supply of thirteen similar bodies on Daimler CVD6 chassis for W. Alexander & Sons Ltd (5681-93) placed in service in June 1951. This was the first manifestation of the fact that Scottish Bus Group companies were able to purchase ECW bodywork at that period, as fellow members of the BTC empire. Alexander generally favoured Leyland vehicles but had included an earlier batch of Daimler CVD6 with Burlingham bodywork amongst its post-war purchases, though the combination of this model with

ECW body remained unique. However, it was barely detectable to the casual onlooker, since the Daimler radiator, slightly taller than the Bristol unit, was concealed by the same type of grille as on the LWL6B – the only difference evident being a slightly higher level to the windscreen bottom edge. The bodies were otherwise to the contemporary standard, with 37 seats. At about the same time, six wartime Guy Arab double-deckers were given new ECW lowbridge bodies (5675-80) for Alexander and the closely-associated Lawson fleet and further similar work was done for Western SMT in 1951-52 on Guy and Daimler CWA6 chassis also dating from the wartime era. In general, however, ECW bodywork did not figure prominently in the Scottish Bus Group's vehicle intake until the mid-'fifties.

The first LS prototype was completed and delivered back to Bristol Tramways & Carriage Co in December 1950. The underfloor engine mounted between the axles required a higher floor line but the overall height was almost exactly the same as the L-type with standard ECW body, at 10ft. 1in. laden, the destination display of similar dimensions being within the roof height and the driver seated at a slightly lower level than the passengers. The windscreen was set noticeably lower than the side windows, a characteristic retained on the production version, though its outline was altered.

The 'Light Saloon'

By 1950, there was strong interest in the underfloor engine position as a means of allowing the whole area of a single-decker to be available for passenger space, except for that required for the driver. There had been pioneer ventures of this kind in the 'thirties but it was the adoption of this layout by the Birmingham & Midland Motor Omnibus Co Ltd (Midland Red) from 1946 for its entire requirements for new single-deckers, of which the chassis were built in its own workshops, that set the pace for the British operating and manufacturing industry.

AEC and Leyland were both developing production underfloor-engined models using their respective 9.6 and 9.8-litre engines and largely intended to cater for export markets where large heavy-duty models were needed, announcements of such designs being made at various stages in 1948-49. Bristol and ECW decided to adopt a different philosophy, bearing in mind the very good fuel economy obtainable from the L-type saloons (with a five-speed gearbox and the Gardner 5LW engine consumption could be up to 14mpg even in hilly terrain) and the ability to tailor a new model to the needs of the Tilling companies in particular and the BTC subsidiaries in general.

Reducing weight is an important factor in reducing running costs and no doubt the earlier work carried out by Beadle and ECW itself in conjunction with Tilling engineers in this direction with their chassisless vehicles was borne in mind. What was now required, however, was a sturdier type of vehicle, capable of giving reliable service with no more than routine attention over long periods on all types of duty, including the most arduous and intensive.

It is clear that the basic concept had been settled by 24th February 1950, for an announcement appearing on that day in *The Commercial Motor* briefly described Bristol-ECW proposals for an integral-construction single-decker making extensive use of light alloy in the underframe

The underframe of the LS was designed to marry up with the body structure, the saloon floor being laid directly upon it and the pillars built on the outriggers. It was not intended to provide more than limited beam strength, that being derived from the body structure as a whole, and hence the main members were quite shallow. Temporary reinforcement was added to allow it to be driven from Bristol to Lowestoft. The example seen here was a prototype and the portions of engine visible appear to be of Gardner design, probably a 4HLW and thus indicating that it was the second example, LSX.002, which became Eastern Counties LL744. The prototypes had underframes constructed in aluminium alloy, but production versions were in steel.

This head-on view of the first prototype shows how the windscreen was set at a level which gave the driver a clear view through the upper, opening, section. The requirement that windscreens were to open, still in force at the time, made screen design and the provision of adequate windscreen wipers quite difficult – note that the nearside wiper cleared the fixed lower section only. The circular Bristol badge was partially surrounded by a curved section reading 'Eastern Coach Works' in cast lettering.

and body, with a choice of four-, five- or six-cylinder horizontal power units. Clearly, planning work must have already reached quite an advanced stage and would have begun in 1949 or possibly even earlier.

The design went ahead on exactly the lines indicated, although the resulting vehicle could best be described as semi-integral. The light underframe, with engine, gearbox,

axles and other units attached was built at Bristol and then driven to Lowestoft with temporary stiffening beams in place. The latter were then removed and the body structure built up by ECW to take advantage of the strength of the framing of the sides and roof in producing a strong yet relatively light complete vehicle. The use of aluminium alloy played a major part in keeping the weight down and

The first LS prototype was of two-door layout, no doubt partly in keeping with BTCC's specification of that layout for some of its existing single-deckers. However, with its 42-seat capacity there was some degree of feeling that this was a 'big' bus, by single-deck standards of the day, and some other operators went on to specify a similar layout for early production models. The rear-end design was adopted with very little change for production models.

The second prototype was delivered to Eastern Counties in June 1950, its underframe having arrived a fortnight after the first vehicle had left, in the previous December. It had a much lower body number, 4255, however, as compared to the first vehicle's 4978, and although ECW body numbers were more in the nature of order reservation numbers (as also applied to some maker's chassis numbers, notably AEC and Daimler) this may suggest that some preliminary work was being done on what became this body at the beginning of the project. These views show the marked difference in levels between the windscreen and side windows, and also the different windscreen design, with upper and lower panes inclined at the same angle, as compared to the Bristol vehicle which had the upper one more inclined, giving the illusion of a curved profile. This vehicle remained in service until 1972, whereas the Bristol one was withdrawn in 1967, but happily both have been preseved.

although the extreme lightness of the earlier Beadle or ECW chassisless buses was not attempted, the 30ft. by 8ft. prototype weighed 5 tons 12cwt unladen, a remarkably low figure in relation to its specification. This was Bristol Tramways No. 2800 (registration number NHU 2) on chassis LSX.001 and with ECW body number 4978, delivered on 12th December 1950. Part of the explanation of the low weight was the use of aluminium alloy in the underframe, and there was probably a slight saving in the use of 7ft. 6in. axles. However, the engine was a horizontal version of the six-cylinder 8.15-litre Bristol AVW, called the LSW and the specification included a five-speed overdrive gearbox, as had been usual on L-type chassis, while the body was of two-door 42-seat type.

It was decided to use steel for the underframe of the production version, which also had 8ft. axles and other changes, but even so the weight of a typical bus with the

Gardner 5HLW engine, which was the more usual choice, was about 6 tons 5cwt. which was about $1\frac{1}{2}$ tons lighter than most early 30ft. x 8ft. buses despite a good standard of interior trim.

A second prototype, using chassis LSX.002 and having a Gardner 4HLW engine and a 42-seat body with front entrance was built for Eastern Counties. It had a considerably earlier body number, 4255, and it seems possible that this might have begun as ECW's part in the initial project development. It entered the Eastern Counties fleet as their LL744 (MAH 744) on 26th June 1951.

As with the Lodekka, there was then a period of assessment of the prototypes together with some modification in design, but with the Lodekka and LS, Bristol and ECW had the basis for the major part of their production for several years, and, with further revisions in design, until well into the 'sixties.

The end of an era. Regular production of the Bristol L series of single-deck chassis ended in September 1951, although a single batch was turned out to special order in 1954. The 1951 body programme included 218 saloon bodies based on LL or LWL chassis delivered between August 1951 and May 1952. They were built in batches 101-105, totalling 182 bodies, all 8ft.-wide, and batch 106, of 36, which were 7ft. 6in. Apart from the adoption of the three-aperture destination display as used from a year earlier on double-deckers, the design was unchanged. The vehicle shown here, Southern Vectis 839 (HDL 283), an LL5G with body 5271, was one of the 7ft. 6in. buses and although built at Lowestoft, three others for this company (5273-5), plus 20 for Crosville (5301-20), were the last bodies built at Irthlingborough.

Chapter four:
Production in the 'fifties

In the aftermath of both the 'political' upheaval which resulted in it becoming part of a State-owned organisation and the major design changes in both double- and single-deck models described in the previous chapter, ECW settled down to a long spell of relative stability. As part of the British Transport Commission, the company's function and output were restricted by the ban on sales to 'outside' operators, but on the other hand the planning of output became even more clear-cut than previously. In general, the Tilling companies were the main and, for a time, virtually the only customers, so the policy of standardisation begun in 1946 could be carried further.

Output did fall somewhat from the peak in the early post-war years, but that was related to the backlog of demand in the aftermath of the war. In the 'fifties the production programmes dipped to low points of 599 in 1954 and 558 in 1958, though 1957 was significantly better at 814, which was repeated exactly for 1962. Although the bus industry was beginning to feel the effects of the increased use of private cars and the drop in evening leisure travel related to the growth in popularity of television, it was still paying its way without subsidy and indeed the BTC's bus-operating companies earned profits which were some help in attempting to offset the losses of the railways.

In a technical sense, ECW had become more involved in the structural engineering of bus design and manufacture, the partnership between Bristol and ECW reaching a stage not parallelled elsewhere. Both concerns supplied almost identical lists of customers with similar quantities of their inter-related products, each literally supported by the other, with only limited work in either case in which the other firm was not involved.

The change in production methods, and the almost-complete winding down of the construction of bodies on Bristol L-type chassis made it logical to close the Irthlingborough works. The last body produced there was No. 5319, a 39-seat saloon on Bristol LL6B chassis delivered to Crosville as KW292 (NFM 48) on 14th May 1952. The works was closed on 31st July 1952 and the

A characteristic of the 8ft-wide saloon body was the divided rear window, reminiscent of the style found on the bodies built on 1946 Leyland PS1 models. This example is Eastern Counties LL732 (LNG 732), with body 5321, delivered in August 1951 and one of four in the 1951 programme for this operator built on 7ft 6in LL5G chassis, delivered in August of that year.

Rare birds indeed were the last four of a delivery of Bristol LWL6B models to United Counties in batch 104, delivered during the first five months of 1952, as they were the only 30ft models to receive bodywork to the 'express' specification, much more familiar in its shorter form. Number 429 (CNH 863), with body 5399, is seen here at Victoria coach station. The seating capacity was very modest at 33, space over the nearside rear wheel arch being used for luggage. United Counties remained wedded to the concept of 'bus'-outline vehicles with coach seats for its express services right up to the RE era.

Rebodying produced some interesting late examples of 27ft 6in saloon bodywork. United Counties had twelve (4962-73) examples for Bristol JO5G chassis, delivered in March-April 1951. Unlike the similar models rebodied in 1949, they also received PV2 radiators. The height problem of this generation of Bristol chassis was less acute than with the double-deck G-type, but there was a very slight difference, possibly amounting to an inch or less, which gave the illusion of a lower radiator than on an L type, as can be seen in the view of body 4962 on number 470 (NV 9651). The last saloon bodies of this length (5444-63) were delivered in December 1951 to Eastern Counties, and had the later type of three-aperture destination display. They were fitted on 20 L4G chassis which had originally carried 1936 bodies by Eastern Counties that had originally been built for 1927 ADC 415 models. Seen here is LL474 (GVF 474) with body 5445.

premises transferred to British Road Services, the road freight transport side of the British Transport Commission's empire, for use as a depot. In fact, it is known that ECW had produced some goods vehicle bodies for BRS at Irthlingborough in the late 'forties but there is no record of how many or what type of bodywork was built.

It is not even certain how many single-deck bus bodies were constructed at Irthlingborough, as there are some discrepancies in the records. However, it is known that at least 549 were produced in the five-year period of construction of the post-war Tilling standard type, generally on new Bristol L-series chassis but including 59 on reconditioned chassis of various types. All were for Tilling operating companies, the records showing that the recipients of these were Bristol Tramways, Caledonian, Crosville, Eastern Counties, Eastern National, Hants & Dorset, Lincolnshire, Southern Vectis, Thames Valley, United, United Counties and West Yorkshire. By far the largest total, outnumbering all the others put together, were for United, which received 368.

Meanwhile, at Lowestoft, the emphasis so far as single-deckers were concerned was switching to underfloor-engined types. While the performance of the two prototype Bristol-ECW LS buses was being assessed and preparations made for volume production, other makes of chassis formed the basis for the first production ECW bodies of this layout.

The first of these also broke new ground in being the first to be built by ECW for London Transport. The fact that both had become part of the State-owned BTC organisation gave rise to speculation that ECW might become a major supplier of bus bodywork to the London Transport Executive, as it had become. In practice this would have been difficult because of restrictions on the total volume of construction BTC could undertake even for its own subsidiaries, quite apart from the agreements reached with other suppliers before the BTC had been set up. However, an urgent need for new and up-to-date coaches for London Transport's private hire fleet had arisen as a result of the plan to hold the Festival of Britain Exhibition in London in 1951, and similar remarks applied to the London-based Tilling Transport coach business.

Parked in the forecourt of the AEC works at Southall, with the company's flag fluttering in the breeze, the first of the London Transport coaches bodied by ECW on AEC Regal IV chassis, RFW1 (LUC 376), with body 5465, awaits delivery to Chiswick in April 1951. The intention was that these vehicles would be used for sightseeing tours or private hire work, which London Transport had been requested to undertake up to a distance of 100 miles of its headquarters by the British Transport Commission – a new departure, as hitherto, LT had been restricted to its specified operating area. This vehicle, and two others, were licensed on the first day of the Festival of Britain on 4th May and the rest followed during that month. The body design was unlike any previous ECW product and indeed more akin to Continental than British practice of the period, with quite severe lines. The livery was dark green and grey, with red lettering.

Accordingly, 20 of the AEC Regal IV underfloor-engined chassis, itself not long in production, were sent to ECW for bodying as what were primarily sightseeing coaches for London Transport. These were ECW body numbers 5465-79, and five more almost identical vehicles, 5480-84, were supplied to Tilling Transport – all were delivered in April-May 1951. They were 30ft. long and 8ft. wide, the latter dimensions causing the LTE examples to be classified RFW – the much larger class of Regal IV vehicles with Metro-Cammell bodywork for more general LTE duties were built to 7ft. 6in. width and were coded RF. The RFW vehicles, as they were universally known, and also the Tilling equivalents, received 39-seat front-entrance bodywork of a type which was to remain unique. Although quite luxurious within, the external lines were much more angular than then usual, not only reverting to a straight waistline and vertical pillars but with quite upright front and rear profiles. The overall effect would have been quite box-like but for the use of curved glass for all four corners, and a comparatively well-rounded roof contour with curved-glass panels above the cantrails.

At the rear, there was a hint of ECW's coach design for the Bristol RE that was to appear at about the time, 1963-4, that the London RFW coaches were withdrawn. Several saw further service, often abroad. Seen here is RFW14, one of the two that survived to be preserved – it had ECW body number 5479 – unusually, they were not in sequence with the fleet numbers. The rear marker lights at roof level were as fitted to the rear wings of contemporary Morris Minor cars.

The five Regal IV coaches for Tilling were virtually identical to the London Transport RFW batch, apart from livery. On both, the full-depth emergency door was on the offside, just ahead of the rear axle. It is said that this had been to facilitate possible hiring of the latter by Tilling for Continental tours, though it is not thought this ever happened. The vehicles would have been quite well suited to such duty, with the refined running of their 9.6-litre engines and preselective transmission, in addition to the well-appointed 39-seat bodywork, with sliding roof and curved glass cantrail windows, though the unladen weight, 8tons 8cwt, was heavier than any of London Transport or the Tilling group's contemporary double-deckers. The vehicle shown, LYM 730, had body 5481.

The next batch of underfloor-engined vehicles to be bodied by ECW gave a clearer indication of what was to follow, as well as being more closely related to the LS prototype design. Cumberland Motor Services Ltd had been a Tilling group company since 1942 but differed from others in that the Meageen family, which had founded it, retained a shareholding which was marginally larger than that held either by Tilling or the LMS Railway. As elsewhere, the railway company deferred to road transport interests and thus the Meageen family remained in control, continuing to favour Leyland chassis. In 1947, an agreement had been signed with Leyland covering Cumberland's requirements for new vehicles for a period up to the mid-'fifties. When the railways were nationalised and then Thomas Tilling sold their interests to BTC in 1948, the combined BTC holding was large enough to take control, but the agreement with Leyland was still in force,

deliveries of vehicles of that make, largely Titan PD2 models with Leyland bodywork, continuing until 1951. The only sign of Tilling influence in the Cumberland fleet at that stage was the rebodying of nine pre-war Leyland TD4 and TD5 models with standard ECW lowbridge bodies in 1950.

However, it was agreed that most of the remaining Cumberland commitment to Leyland would be discharged by the ordering of some batches of the recently introduced Royal Tiger underfloor-engined model. Of these, five received ECW 45-seat saloon bodies for Cumberland's own use, being delivered in March 1952. These bodies, though based on a conventional chassis, had quite a strong resemblance to the LS prototypes, with the same style of windscreen, with quite sharply curved lower edge. Other Royal Tiger chassis were diverted to United, as mentioned on the next page.

These mock-ups were used to develop the original LS coach body. The registration NHU 2 was that of the LS prototype bus, but was probably used here because a plate of the right style with this number was 'lying about'.

LS models in volume

By that date, Bristol had switched from vertical front-engined models to the horizontal underfloor engine layout for its main single-decker production. Manufacture of the LL and LWL chassis ended in September 1951, though there was to be one further batch a few years later. The first production type LS underframe, with chassis number 89.001, was delivered on 12th November 1951 and the body (6301) completed in April 1952. This body number coming after those of some 105 production coaches built subsequently suggests that it may have been issued after the initial work had been done on an experimental basis. It was an LS6G 39-seat coach built for Crosville, receiving fleet number UG294 and registered as OFM 666, though used for a time by Bristol largely for test purposes and not finally delivered to the operator until nearly a year later, on 25th April 1953.

The LS coach body design, though structurally similar to the bus equivalent, was new in terms of styling, quite different to the London Transport RFW and with front and rear having more generously curved lines than the bus version – mock ups were used to develop it. The windscreen glass had a curved profile and there were separate corner glasses having double curvature to conform to the required shape. At that date, it was still a legal requirement that the windscreen of a public service vehicle must be capable of being opened (so as to improve vision in dense fog) and so the main panels, very unusually, were designed to wind down. At the rear the contours of a generously curved dome was matched by curved glass in the rear window panels. Basically the principle of standardised livery was

The prototype Bristol LS coach, Crosville UG294 (OFM 666), seen soon after completion in April 1952, undergoing brake tests alongside the River Severn in Bristol – it was not delivered to the operator until a year later. The body design was adopted unchanged for early production models and, with progressive modifications, was to continue in production until 1961.

continued and almost all early LS coaches were delivered in cream, with maroon, green or black relief. General deliveries of LS coaches got under way in June 1952, the first example (5769) going to Southern Vectis on 13th June 1952 as their No. 303 (JDL 44) and soon examples were to be seen in many of the Tilling fleets. A version of this body design was fitted to four Leyland Royal Tiger chassis and delivered to United for its London-Newcastle service in July 1952, the body numbers (5671-74) following

The 1952 coach design put ECW into the forefront of styling leaders, and the blend of smooth lines and neat detailing looked most impressive in scenes such as this, as South Midland 79 (SFC 565) stands in the arrival bay of Victoria coach station, London in July 1952. It had been among the first production examples from the initial batch 122, delivered the previous month. Like most of the type, it was on LS6G chassis, the length of the six-cylinder Gardner engine no longer being a problem when mounted under the floor. South Midland specified 37-seat capacity, giving quite generous seat spacing for its Oxford-London service; other operators with longer routes usually favoured 39 or 41.

Royal Blue was really no more than a marketing name for a network of services to the south west of England, but its coaches, owned by Western National or Southern National, had a distinctive air all their own. Unusually for that period, the LS design was adapted to incorporate a roof-mounted luggage rack, but this was neatly done in a way that, if anything, added to the glamour. Seen here is Western National 1279 (LTA 867), the first of that company's initial batch of seven LS6G with 41-seat body 6294. Southern National had a similar batch, the two combining to make up ECW batch 125, delivered in July-September 1952.

on from the Cumberland buses. A further five similar vehicles followed in 1953 (7021-25). One AEC Regal IV chassis which had been ordered for South Midland also received a body of the LS coach style (5772).

Manufacture of the production version of the LS bus also started in 1952, deliveries beginning with United BU1, 3 and 4 (PHN 830, 832 and 833) on 10th October 1952. (Body Nos. 5704/6/7). In this case the design was substantially similar to that of the prototypes although the windscreen shape was altered both in outline, now with a basically horizontal lower edge, and in being raked to a reduced extent. The rear window was reduced in depth to accommodate a full-sized destination display when specified, this having become of the three-panel type in accordance with Tilling's revised standard by that period. Normal seating capacity was 45 with front entrance, though some operators took delivery of 43-seat two-door versions. Bodies of this type were also fitted on five Leyland Royal Tiger and one Guy Arab UF chassis for United in 1953.

There was also a 'semi-coach' version, roughly comparable with the 'express' version of the L-type body

An oddity in more ways than one was South Midland 85 (SFC 571). The AEC Regal IV chassis, of type 9821E, very like the London and Tilling examples, had been ordered when South Midland was in the Red & White group and at that time, standardising on AEC coaches. The body was built as one of the 35 in batch 123 and largely as produced for the LS (it being significant that 'chassis' and 'integral' were regarded as sufficiently similar to be batched together) and the vehicle delivered in August 1952. The windscreen opened conventionally, perhaps initially because of the radiator header tank and filler of the AEC chassis below it, but a similar system was adopted for the 36 LS coaches in batch 124 built early in 1953.

in having coach seats within the bus body shell, though in this case not having quite so much of a coach character in terms of exterior trim. This was generally a 41-seat front-entrance vehicle, though there was a 39-seat two-door version favoured by Wilts & Dorset and United Counties for a time. In general, the full coaches were of LS6G type and most of the early buses were LS5G, with the semi-coaches of either variant, though there were exceptions to this general pattern, including a limited proportion of LS6B, mainly coaches; the emphasis was more comprehensively on Gardner engines than was so with front-engined models.

Soon after the production version of the LS coach entered service, it was discovered that the windscreen design was not satisfactory. The wind-down windscreen was used on the first batches of vehicles, but then a modified version was introduced towards the end of the 1952 programme with the upper part of both main panels arranged to open outwards as normal at the time. It was then decided to adopt a more extensively redesigned and simpler front-end, with the main windscreen panels widened to eliminate the curved corner sections, for the 1953 programme (except that the second batch of United Royal Tigers, delivered in May of that year, retained the wind-down windscreens). The first example of the re-designed coach (6963) again went to Southern Vectis, being delivered on 15th May 1953 as their No. 308 (JDL 756). Although the individual windscreen panels were of flat glass, they were set at angles which conformed quite closely to the curved profile and the overall effect was, at least in the view of many observers, neater. It also had the practical merit that the entrance door could be significantly wider especially if, as was common practice, the door was hinged to open outwards, as on a private car. An alternative inward-opening version of hinged door was optional but this did create some loss of width in opening.

The switchover from front-engined to underfloor-engined single-deckers had become almost complete during 1952-53 so far as ECW production was concerned – the 1953 programme included no fewer than 367 of the LS type in bus, express carriage or coach versions, while the L-type had dropped out of the picture, although revived on a small scale for one fleet the following year.

Perhaps the most familiar country bus of the 'fifties was the Bristol-ECW LS5G and here photographer G. H. F. Atkins perfectly captures the scene at Newark bus station in June 1953, as Lincolnshire 978 (JFU 294), new the previous November, departs for Lincoln, with two 1936 Leyland Tiger TS7 buses, rebodied post-war by Burlingham, in the background. It had numerically the second production LS bus body, 5695, among the first delivered from batch 118, the first 'general' batch of 30 of the type. United's initial 30 in batch 117, some of which had been completed first, differed slightly in having a manually-operated door. The standard version seated 45, as here, and the design differed from the two prototypes in having a more nearly rectangular windscreen with top edge slightly higher, causing the roof line to be swept up at the front to accomodate the three-aperture roof box usually fitted. The 1952 programme included 95 LS saloon bodies, mainly built in batches 117-119 and 121, with two odd examples in later batches, but 775 of the type were to be built before production stopped in 1957, with no more than minor modifications and largely of the standard 45-seat pattern.

The idea that 30ft single-deckers should have two doorways only took root to a limited extent, but eleven of the 1952 programme LS buses were of this layout and all built in batch 121, including United Counties 441 (HBD 630), an LS5G with body 5740, seating 43. It is seen in Nottingham in May 1953, having been placed in service the previous winter. Somewhat surprisingly, it was pressed into duty on the London service, probably on the basis of being quite new at the time but liable to upset passengers looking for coach standards. The LS5G was relatively 'civilised' by comparison with some lightweight models of the day, but the seat pitch was very tight for a journey of over 100 miles and the Gardner 5HLW took on a rougher character at speed.

Even more surprising in retrospect was the construction of 40 out of the 51 'express' LS saloons constructed in batches 118-21 in the 1952 programme with two-door layout, using the same type of jack-knife door as the bus version. Wilts & Dorset was the largest user, with 28 LS6G, but United Counties had twelve LS5G, followed by five more on the less common LS6B in the 1953 programme. One of the latter, 470 (JBD 988) with body 6873, dating from later that year, is seen entering Victoria Coach Station in London. The seats, for 39 passengers, were of coach type and other differences included the omission of the top strip in the front destination display, with level roof line in consequence. The livery style and addition of polished beading gave a touch of coach appearance, but the overall effect was more utilitarian than the L-type express model.

77

In 1952-53, United resumed its pre-war practice of using Leyland coaches for its London services. Four Royal Tiger PSU1/15 models were included in ECW's 1951 programme, emerging with bodies (5671-4) of similar style to those just introduced for the LS, in July 1952. Five more (bodies 7021-5) followed in May 1953, being the first coaches to be completed in the 1953 programme. The two batches were generally similar, but the 1952 vehicles were unusual at that date in having two half-drop windows on each side, whereas the 1953 version had sliding vents in all the main side windows, even adding one in the entry door. Three illuminated cantrail panels on each side carried 'Tyne-Tees-Thames-Service' lettering, and an illuminated 'United' sign at the front was raised in position on the 1953 coaches to create an effect that had been traditional on United long-distance coaches previously. The original 1952 pattern of windscreen was retained, however, and this view of LUT7 (RHN 770), with body 7023, in Doncaster for a meal stop, shows the nearside portion wound down.

The 1953 single-deck programme included 228 LS buses built in batches 137-142, 159 and 161. Included were 40 for Red & White, which had begun to take standard Bristol-ECW products following its acquisition by BTC in 1950, though unusual at that stage in selecting the LS6G for bus duties. Uniquely, they had nearside fuel and water fillers. Seen here is U2654 (MAX 126) with body 6921. Most operators favoured the 45-seat single-door version, as here, but batch 142 comprised 24 more two-door examples. In addition, there were five Leyland Royal Tiger (7016-20) and one Guy Arab UF (7041) for United, all of which received LS-style bus bodies in March-April 1953, and two LS were returned to Bristol untrimmed and painted in grey primer for experimental purposes. One of these (with body 6858) had a Commer T.S.3 two-stroke diesel engine and the other (6951, with lightweight features) an AEC AH410 engine and AEC gearbox. Both were later completed and delivered to Bristol's operating department in 1955.

A redesigned windscreen using flat glass and opening in the then conventional way was adopted for the 123 Bristol-ECW LS coaches of the 1953 programme, built in batches 143 (ten for Royal Blue) and 145-9 (other fleets) between May of that year and September 1954. The effect was, if anything, even more sleek looking, and a further benefit was the wider door. Western National took vehicles with glazed cantrail panels for its tours, 1351 (OTT 33) with body 7101 of batch 147, one of three LS6G delivered in the summer of 1953 being shown.

From a bodywork point of view, possibly the most interesting part of the 84 London Transport GS-type 26-seat single-deckers on Guy 'special' chassis for use on quiet country routes was the rear, and the way in which the style of the contemporary fleet of full-sized RF-class single deckers was echoed. At the front, the ingenious use of the Briggs sheet-metalwork as being made for Ford goods models, modified by a grille surmounted by the Red Indian mascot favoured by Guy, had been explored in a mock-up at LT's Chiswick works. The end result was perhaps the most attractive small bus of its period. Although the Perkins engine was not entirely trouble-free, former LT engineer Colin Curtis regards them as superior to many of today's midi buses. The first one, GS1 (MXX 301), with body 6347, is seen just before delivery in October 1953, and GS80 is seen in Windsor soon after entering service, alongside one of the well-liked 10T10 coaches of 1938, ending its days on local services.

Output of the LS types ran more typically at about 200 to 250 a year through the mid-'fifties, tailing off in 1957, by which date nearly 1,400 had been built.

ECW became involved in the construction of bodywork for vehicles in a lighter category, however, in one case as a one-off and in the other a further manifestation of contact with London Transport.

The first was a consequence of the takeover by Eastern Counties of an independent operator, B. Beeston & Sons of East Bergholt, for whom an Albion Victor FT39L chassis had been ordered. On it was built a 35-seat rear-entrance saloon body (6177), basically to the Tilling standard for front-engined models though having a full-fronted cab and a rather higher build to suit the chassis, derived from contemporary Albion goods models of similar basic design. It was delivered in June 1953.

More significant in its implications was London Transport's order for 84 bodies of 26-seat capacity on a specially-developed Guy chassis. These were to replace that operator's fleet of Leyland Cub 20-seat buses dating from 1935-36. There had been a proposal to retain these and rebody them, ECW preparing drawings accordingly, but it then became known that Leyland was withdrawing spares availability. New chassis of suitable design were

sought and the choice fell on a hybrid of the Guy concern's Vixen and Otter models, using a Perkins diesel engine, classified GS (Guy Special) by LTE. It was of bonneted layout and it was decided to use the bonnet and front wing assembly as then being made by Briggs Motor Bodies Ltd for the Ford Thames normal-control models – a mock-up of the complete front end was built at London Transport's Chiswick works.

The ECW body was based on standard Lowestoft constructional methods but looked very different, partly

Significantly, the Tilling group generally did not favour the purchase of buses with fewer than 35 seats in the post-war period, despite the many deep rural services its companies operated. It was perhaps surprising that an Albion Victor FT39L chassis which had been ordered by an operator whose business was purchased by Eastern Counties but not delivered until after the take-over was taken into stock, but the model would accept a body of this capacity, and the result was as shown. The vehicle was delivered in June 1953, becoming the operator's N973 (NAH 973), with body 6177. The higher build of the Albion, derived from a goods model, can be seen by comparison with a Bristol SC – described later in this chapter – parked behind.

Spare capacity combined with the ban on 'outside' work led to the construction of Bristol goods vehicles, for the first time since a 'twenties design had gone out of production, and for ECW to build cabs for them, the customer being British Road Services, another part of the BTC empire. The HG6L was a conventional eight-wheeler of the period, though the choice of engine, the Leyland O.600, was significant in the light of later events; the reason at that time was probably that the Gardner 6LW, excellent unit that it was, had rather limited power for a 24-ton-gross vehicle. ECW's timber-framed cab was also quite orthodox, but the use of the instantly recognisable 'traditional' Bristol radiator outline, rather than that of the prototype Lodekka buses, as might have been expected at the time, set a precedent for the future. A BRS (Southern) example is seen when working in Bristol.

because of the layout – ECW had not built on a bonneted chassis since 1940 and even then not in comparable numbers. However, details of the finish and particularly the external appearance from the rear were designed to resemble those of the RF-class single-deckers on AEC Regal IV chassis then entering service in large numbers with London Transport.

Another ECW product of that period was the batch of cabs and flat-platform bodies built for the Bristol eight-wheel heavy goods vehicle chassis produced as another consequence of both Bristol and ECW ownership as British Transport Commision subsidiaries. British Road Services, as BTC's road haulage division, placed part of its vehicle requirements within the organisation. Initially a prototype cab and platform body were constructed and these were mounted on chassis number 88.001 by ECW itself. It is not known whether the cab and/or the body were given body numbers but the resulting vehicle was first registered on 1st November 1952. ECW then produced 49 cabs based on the prototype, all of timber-framed construction. Its radiator grille outline, of traditional Bristol outline, though larger than the K or L style and applied directly to the front of the cab, established a principle followed in many later passenger models.

The cabs did not form part of ECW's general production programme but received body numbers G222-270, the implication being that this series had been used for previous ECW goods vehicle bodies or cabs, possibly including those built at Irthlingborough, but no record has survived to confirm this. They were delivered between 12th December 1952 and 1st April 1953 and mounted on chassis 88.002/004-51 at Bristol's Chatsworth Road assembly factory. Bristol records also show that ECW built a further 39 flat-platform bodies at Irthlingborough,

also sent to Bristol for mounting, but in this case at the main Brislington works.

The Lodekka in quantity

Double-decker output continued to be based on the Bristol KSW chassis, apart from occasional rebodying work, until 1953 when the first Lodekka models of the production LD type appeared. Indeed even then only a pre-production batch of six LD vehicles appeared between March and May of that year, and volume deliveries from the 1953 programme of 170 production Lodekka did not begin until early in 1954. Originally these had been programmed as KSW lowbridge buses but switched to the new model. However, KSW production continued alongside the Lodekka on a scale which, though diminished to some degree, was still substantial until the mid-'fifties. The emphasis switched to the highbridge type, of which 106, including 70 for Bristol Tramways, were built in the 1954 programme. Output of lowbridge bodies dwindled to 33 in that programme, being built for United Counties and Thames Valley (the latter receiving the last five, 7473-77, in 1955), ceasing thereafter apart from a small batch for rebodying. The design of body for the KSW chassis did not significantly alter during its production run save for the 'staggered' lowbridge seating shown on page 82. Among the more significant variants were lowbridge versions with seating to coach standards and platform doors, notably for Thames Valley.

Inevitably the spotlight of publicity was on the Lodekka, however, and even though not available outside the BTC sector, the bus industry in general was impressed with its design. Though the two prototypes had established the design principle, considerable revision to the appearance

The first of the six pre-production Bristol Lodekka LD6B models, chassis number 100.001, went back to Bristol Tramways & Carriage Co after completion of the body (7108) by ECW on 15th March 1953, and is seen soon after, parked by the River Severn. Although the principles established by the two prototypes of 1949/50 had been shown to be sound, extensive redesign of both chassis and body had been carried out. The appearance had greatly altered, and though the visual problem of reconciling a low waistline with a taller bonnet remained, the execution was much neater. The concept of the 'three-quarter width' bonnet introduced for Birmingham City Transport's 'new look' of 1950 had been adopted, and the coarse radiator grille slats of these six vehicles seemed to owe something to that design, but the Bristol radiator outline first seen on the HG goods model gave more 'character'.

was evident in the pre-production and production version. By 1953, the concealed radiator type of double-deck front-end had come into widespread favour, strongly influenced by the 1950 Birmingham City Transport 'new look' design which was adopted almost unaltered as a standard by Daimler and Guy. The Lodekka LD-type adopted the same principle of what might be termed three-quarter width bonnet assembly, with a rounded front cowl projecting ahead of the cab front panel, but the application

of the same style of polished aluminium border to the radiator grille as used on the HG goods cabs gave a distinctive Bristol identity.

The same effect of a low-built version of a highbridge body remained and this made the bonnet assembly still appear rather bulky but the disproportionate effect of the prototypes had largely gone. Moreover the body itself was both tidier in detail and had more flowing lines than either of the prototype versions. The front end had a more curved

The pre-production Lodekka vehicles did their stint as 'demonstrators'. Here Crosville ML661 (RFM 406), with the second chassis, 100.002, and body 6551 is seen in Nottingham (Mount Street), working on hire to Midland General in May 1953, when only a month old. The second Lodekka prototype had also visited Midland General in 1951, as shown on page 56, but the new model was not yet available in quantity and a batch of fifteen Bristol KSW6G buses with ECW highbridge bodywork, one of which is visible behind the Lodekka, had been purchased earlier in 1953 to replace Notts & Derby trolleybuses. These were the first Bristol buses in this fleet.

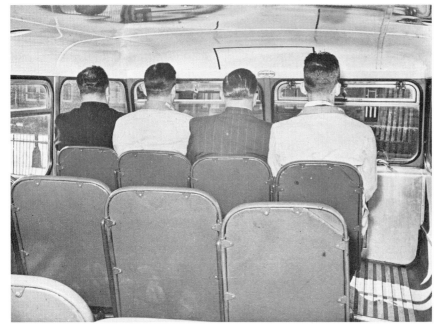

Ironically, just as the lowbridge double-decker was about to be made obsolete by the Lodekka, an ingenious alteration was made to reduce one of its disadvantages. In 1952, the West Yorkshire Road Car Co devised this staggered seating arrangement for the upper deck, trying the idea out on a KSW delivered the previous year, 830 (ECW body 5543). It was an adaptation of an idea sometimes found in coaches of the 'thirties, but the skewing of the seats to face slightly to the nearside helped to economise on space. The photograph shows how the shoulders of passengers could overlap slightly, avoiding the discomfort of four people on a bench seat of barely adequate width, though it also illustrates how forward vision was impeded in a lowbridge bus. In the 1952 programme, 227 lowbridge bodies (5782-988, 6083-102) were built on KSW chassis in batches 96 and 107-113, some of which also included buses from the 1951 or 1953 programmes. Most of those in batches 112-3, built from April 1953, had staggered seating. In the 1953 programme, output of lowbridge buses was winding down, 88 being built on KSW chassis (numbers more fragmented, but extending up to 7121) and apart from two for United Welsh in batch 111, all the others, in batches 113, 126/7, had staggered seating.

Platform doors were another feature beginning to become more common on ECW double-deckers, after their initial introduction on Thames Valley's Service B vehicles in January 1951. In the 1952 programme, lowbridge bodies for Bristol Country Services (5 vehicles), Bath Tramways (5) and Eastern National (3) were so fitted. The last-mentioned, dating from Spring 1953, were for the Braintree-London service, and thus analagous to the Thames Valley version, though rather more basic, on KSW5G chassis and with 55 bus seats. Seen here is 2365, originally numbered 4190, with body 5876. This feature added 3cwt to the vehicle's unladen weight. Also fitted with platform doors in that year's programme were four highbridge bodies on KSW chassis for Bristol Country Services and five for Lincolnshire. In the 1953 programme, doors were fitted to fifteen lowbridge KSWs for Wilts & Dorset and on six highbridge for United plus two more for Lincolnshire.

The highbridge-bodied KSW was represented in the 1952 programme by 94 examples (5989-6082) and in the 1953 programme by a further 95 (6508-22, 6631/2/72-734, 7026-40), which were to be found in batches 99/100, 114-6 and 134-6. The design, with 60 seats as standard, continued unchanged from the 1951 version – the photographs on this page show the glazing of the short bay just in front of the platform introduced at that stage. Seen here is one of the fifteen (bodies 7026-40) supplied to replace the Notts & Derby trolleybuses in April 1953. They were owned by the Nottinghamshire & Derbyshire Traction Co, but the licences of the replacement services were joint with Midland General, effectively the parent company. These concerns were allowed more freedom than other Tilling companies, retaining their handsome blue and cream livery and the destination layout shown. The chassis was the KSW6G, increasingly popular from 1952, the Gardner 6LW engine making full use of the KS-series bonnet length – with the 5LW or Bristol AVW, the last 6in was filled with 'fresh air'. The placing of the rear access hole gives a visual means of identification.

This view of the third Lodekka in the 1953 pre-production batch of six, Hants & Dorset 1337 (LRU 67) with body 6616, delivered in April, shows how the lines of the new body design were more curvaceous than any of ECW's earlier post-war double-deckers. Proportions had improved greatly compared to the two rather ungainly prototypes and though the new grille was still on the large side, this was to be subject to revision later. Just how to deal with the cab side seemed to remain in doubt, and these particular vehicles carried the waist moulding horizontally but the window line had a 'kick-up' evidently to avoid the panelling appearing too shallow over the mudguard. The bus is seen in Bournemouth bus station in July 1967, by then having received the projecting louvre over the windscreen that was something of a Hants & Dorset 'trade mark', as well as losing the upper cream band and the top line of the destination display. All six were bodied as batch 128.

profile than any ECW double-decker since the pre-war highbridge design, and the uneven pillar spacing gave way to a '4¹/₄'-bay layout, the chassis outriggers having been repositioned to allow equal-length glazing for all the main side windows on each deck, each being provided with a top sliding portion.

The six pre-production prototypes, all LD6B models, were to have been built as a single batch with consecutive body numbers 7108-13, but, in the event, only 7108 was used for the first vehicle, based on chassis 100.001 and delivered back to Bristol as L8133 on 15th March 1953. The remainder took the first numbers that had already been allocated to batches of low-height double-deckers for the operators concerned, going out as Crosville ML661 (body 6551) on 2nd April 1953, Hants & Dorset 1337 (6616) on 21st April 1953, United Counties 950 (6533) on

27th April 1953, West Yorkshire DX2 (6660) on 14th May 1953 and Western National 1863 (7179) on 22nd May 1953. All six operators were subsequently to build up substantial Lodekka fleets, but these vehicles were also to be used as 'demonstrators' and to gain experience before volume manufacture started.

Series production deliveries duly began in February 1954, this time with the usual range of engine options, including LD6G (the layout having been designed to accept the Gardner 6LW) and LD5G as well as LD6B, and with some body variants. The top of the front cowl was more curved and the grille more finely slatted but the body otherwise was unchanged in outline. The provision of platform doors was an option frequently specified, as opposed to the relative rarity on the KSW. Seating capacity was at first generally 58, though Crosville took eight of its

Early production Lodekka models showed only minor changes from the pre-production batch – a grille with finer slats, a bonnet top with a more rounded shape, and the beading on the cab side following the curve of the glazing. As many of the early orders had been changed from lowbridge KSW models, the body numbering of the 1953 programme production run of 170 was very fragmented, with the lowest at 6534 and spreading up to 7203. They were built in batches 129-33 and 151, delivery beginning in February 1954 and lasting for a year. Seen here is Hants & Dorset 1349 (NEL 25), an LD6G with body 6628, this being in the same run of numbers as the pre-production example for the same fleet shown above and typical of the pattern around this period. It was built in batch 133 and delivered in November 1954, being in substantially original condition when photographed.

Crosville chose the Lodekka as the basis for eight special vehicles for the Liverpool-Llandudno express service, delivered in July-August 1954. They were LD6B models and the bodies (6565-72, included with standard examples in batch 131) were fitted with semi-coach seats for 50, with a removable luggage rack which allowed capacity to go up to 52 if required. At the rear, in addition to having platform doors (a regular option for the Lodekka from the beginning of production), they had a straight staircase with emergency door on the offside, the lower-deck rear window being a single rectangular pane. The opening windows were of combined sliding and hopper type. Originally they were in a coach-style cream and black livery, but in 1958 they were put into the green and cream style shown here and the front destination enlarged to the standard type.

early delivery as 50-seat coaches with a straight staircase layout and extra luggage rack accommodation for use on its express services between Merseyside and North Wales. Southern Vectis had 21 buses with luggage racks over the rear wheel arches and a 54-seat capacity and Cumberland had 58 high-backed seats fitted to its first five Lodekkas (the first Bristol double-deckers in the fleet) to counter the introduction of new railcars on a local British Railways line.

The careful development of the Lodekka paid off, for despite its unorthodox design, it soon became recognised as a reliable as well as logical solution to the low-height bus problem. The 1954 programme total of 167 LD vehicles was slightly down on that set in 1953, but thereafter rose steadily to a peak of 417 LD models in the 1957 programme, reducing again subsequently as other Lodekka variants began to appear.

Various minor changes were made, perhaps most obviously the adoption of a shallower radiator grille outline from about the middle of the 104th chassis sanction, reaching operators around the end of May 1955 – not infrequently earlier vehicles were later modified similarly as a result of minor accident repairs. The seating capacity became 60 at about the same time, although Bristol Tramways, Mansfield District and Midland General continued to specify 58 seats until the introduction of the FS- type Lodekka in 1960.

Although Bristol and ECW had thus effectively switched over to the Lodekka and LS as their principal types of double- and single-deck models in production by 1954, the previous generation of models did not die away as rapidly as might have been expected. Admittedly, the Bristol L-type chassis was thought to have 'died' by 1952 in terms of deliveries to operators.

The end of ECW lowbridge body construction, after a long period when it had been the main builder of the type, came in the 1954 programme. There were 33 lowbridge bodies on new chassis, all Bristol KSW6B, 24 for Thames Valley (7204-15 and 7466-77, the latter with platform doors) and nine for United Counties (7216-24). The first 28 were built in batch 150 between August and October 1954, but the last five for Thames Valley were not batched, probably because they were built separately about a year later. Most were of 55-seat capacity with the staggered seating layout on the upper deck, but 7466-71 were the last of Thames Valley's coach-seated vehicles with a capacity of 53. The first of the Thames Valley vehicles, 726 (JRX 801) with body 7204 is seen in company with a 1958 Lodekka, clearly showing the relative height comparison.

Despite its general devotion to the principle of standardisation, ECW built a surprising variety of double-deck designs in the early to mid 'fifties, even if all instantly recognisable as Lowestoft products. In addition to the Lodekka and KSW lowbridge and highbridge versions, themselves quite divergent in character, rebodying widened the range. In the 1952 programme, the rebodying of Bristol K-type chassis of the wartime W1 and W2 sanctions of 1944-5 with 26ft by 7ft 6in lowbridge bodies (6303-27), almost identical to the 1947-50 pattern, was carried out the following year for Crosville, which took 22 K6A and Southern Vectis, whose four examples had Gardner 5LW engines – all received PV2 radiators. The three-aperture destination gave a clue to their later construction, and a minor detail which changed the appearance quite noticeably was the omission of the weather strip over the windscreen. Seen still looking smart when in service at Llangollen in April 1962 was Crosville DKA181, as it had become, originally MB181 (FFM 337).

Western SMT sent nineteen double-deckers to be rebodied in the winter of 1952-3, taking body numbers 6328-46 which followed on from the the batches illustrated above. The four oldest were Albion Venturer CX19 models dating from 1938 that had been taken over with the business of Youngs' Bus Service of Paisley in 1951 and originally had English Electric highbridge bodies. Western had built up something of a collection of Venturers, new and acquired, but it was noteworthy that these fourteen-year-old vehicles were considered worthy of new bodies, lowbridge as then usual for Western. The design of the CX19 altered little over the years, and so the end result was quite similar to the examples on the same model built for Red & White and United Welsh in 1948, though the cab design was closer to the KSW pattern and seating was for 53. Seen here is N2113 (XS 4774).

The remainder of Western SMT's order consisted of fifteen Leyland Titan PD1 models that dated from as recently as 1948-9, six having originated with Western's Greenock Motor Services subsidiary. The original lowbridge bodies were built by Strachans to a newly-introduced metal-framed design which deteriorated very rapidly in service, to the point that replacement after a mere four years or so proved the only answer. As with the Albions, they were rebodied to 26ft by 7ft 6in five-bay 53-seat pattern, but in this case a revised cab design gave them a quite markedly different appearance to the PD1 models bodied from new. The square-cut front dash panel characteristic of this chassis remained, but introducing a slight step immediately above it allowed the windscreen to follow the body contour more tidily. Seen here at Newton Mearns in August 1964 is D508 (CCS 406), with body 6335. Alongside is one of the 1947 batch of 45 PD1 models with original Leyland bodies dating from 1947, all still in service at the time.

The remaining new double-deck bodies on existing chassis in the 1952 programme were to the 'half-way house' pattern, five bay and with pre-1950-style cab profile, but 8ft wide and with curved-waist bulkhead, mounted on Bristol K chassis for Tilling fleets. Eastern Counties took six 56-seat highbridge (6443-8), of which LKH32 (FAH 108) with body 6446 is seen above left, and twelve 55-seat lowbridge (6431-42), LK41 (FNG 399) with body 6435 being shown above right. In all cases the 1944-5 chassis received Gardner 5LW engines. Another dozen lowbridge of this type (6449-60) went to United Counties on 1940 K5G chassis that had originally operated for Eastern National.

Rebodying in the 1954 programme was very limited, but a special version of the 4¼-bay 60-seat highbridge body was produced to suit 26ft Bristol K-type chassis. Two, of 7ft 6in width, were built that year for Brighton Hove & District (7762/3), the chassis being W1-sanction K6A models converted with 5LW engines as well as receiving PV2 radiators etc. This view of BH&D 6375 (CPM 17) shows how the design was adapted to the shorter bonnet, the foremost side window in the upper deck being similarly shortened, and the rear end was also reduced in length.

The ten bodies built for Hants & Dorset in 1954 (7590-9) were also of this 4¼-bay type, being based on K5G chassis dating from 1938-40. The first six had detachable roof structures, the first 'convertibles' built by ECW since 1938, and were painted in cream with green mudguards in H&D's usual manner for such vehicles. In this view of 1034 (ERU 262) with body 7595, the shortened cab window ahead of the driver's door is evident.

The 1955 programme included 37 instances of rebodying, small in proportion to work on new chassis, but bringing yet more variety. The 'foreshortened' 4¼-bay highbridge body was represented by eleven examples for the York-West Yorkshire fleet (8350-60), based on K5G chassis of 1939 origin but rebuilt on new frames and re-registered, a comparatively rare course of action in those days. The first four seated 56 but the rest 55, unusually for highbridge buses. Number YDG84 (OWT 197) with body 8352 is seen passing through the old city wall. Four more similar bodies, but seating 60, were built for Brighton Hove & District on K6A W3-type chassis that had been new to London Transport in 1946 but had run for BH&D with their original Duple bodies since purchase in 1953. These retained their AEC engines and had been fitted with PV2 radiators from new.

Midland General took delivery of seven 7ft. 6in.-wide highbridge five-bay 58-seat bodies, six (8397-8402) being on Guy Arab II chassis with Gardner 6LW engines dating from 1945. They had previously carried Roe utility lowbridge bodies. No. 105 (JNU 683) is seen in Mansfield in March 1956. The other similar body (8249) was for an AEC Regent III of the 9612E type with 9.6-litre engine and preselective gearbox, new to the associated Mansfield District company in 1948 but transferred to Notts & Derby as part of the trolleybus replacement fleet in 1953. Its Weymann body was severely damaged in an accident in November 1954 and thus created the only instance of an ECW body on a Regent III chassis, the somewhat KSW-like cab, adjusted for the taller AEC radiator, producing quite a neat effect. Note the variety of other buses in this view of 316 (JVO 942) in Nottingham in February 1956.

Rounding off the sequence of double-deck rebodying in 1955 were nine 55-seat lowbridge bodies (8418-26) which reverted to the pre-1950 style and were built on Bristol K-type chassis dating from 1942-5, six for the Western National fleet and three for Southern National. Among them was the K5G chassis that had carried the original highbridge prototype body (8063 of 'Series 1', illustrated on page 19) which established the post-war standard, 350 (JTA 271). Although this meant the loss of a historic ECW product, it was perhaps fitting that it should be replaced by one of the last bodies to almost the same design (8423 of Series 2), albeit lowbridge – the chassis received a PV2 radiator, losing its intermediate-height original. It is seen here in Plymouth bus station in 1970.

Wilts & Dorset Motor Services Ltd placed an order for fifteen further Bristol LWL5G, however, and bodies for these (7605-19) were completed to the standard 30ft. by 8ft. 39-seat design as last built two years previously, and delivered in October-November 1954. Their delivery caused some surprise as this operator had already received some 37 LS saloons of the 39-seat express carriage type, but it was felt that vehicles of this pattern would incur excessively high maintenance costs on various minor roads in the company's area. They were not quite the last saloon bodies of this style to be built as six of the 30ft. by 7ft. 6in. version were constructed on lengthened L5G chassis dating from 1938-42 for the Western and Southern National companies in 1955.

Rather similarly, there was a revival of what was basically the 1951-style curved-waist coach as built for front-engined chassis, though in this case all were rebodyings. The United concern had operated a special fleet of ten single-deckers for a service operated along the sea front at Scarborough since 1935. The initial fleet had

been bodied by Plaxton at its works in the town and were full-fronted vehicles with centre entrance layout and prominent destination boxes above the doorway and on the opposite side, based on ADC 425 chassis dating from 1928. The inspiration for the layout seems likely to have been the introduction of a new fleet of single-deck centre-entrance trams at Blackpool. Scarborough, seeking to promote itself as a rival seaside resort, persuading United to provide something comparable. The Plaxton bodies were transferred to 1938 Leyland Tiger TS8 chassis in 1949 and soldiered on until the 1956 season. A 'fresh start' was made in 1957, when ten Bristol L5G chassis of 1946/7 vintage were lengthened to 30ft. and fitted with new 8ft. bodies (9993-10002) based on the 1951 coach design but again featuring centre entrance and prominent side indicators. They had 39 bus-type seats within.

The final bodies of basically the same type were five (10012-16) based on 1949 AEC Regal III 9621E-type chassis for the London-based Tilling fleet. These originally had Strachans full-fronted bodywork, having been built

Wilts & Dorset caused widespread surprise by placing a special order for fifteen more Bristol LWL5G single-deckers with standard 39-seat rear-entrance bodies two years after the type was taken out of production. Bristol produced the chassis as a special sanction, the 103rd, and ECW built the bodies (7605-19) as batch 166 – no changes in design were discernible. New full-sized front-engined single-deck buses of any make had become very rare, and the rear-entrance layout even more so. It is understood that the L-type was thought better suited to rural routes, though in that case the choice of the 30ft by 8ft version is a little difficult to understand – there seems to have been no significant criticism of the LS. It certainly made life more interesting for the enthusiast, though in the event these vehicles, delivered in October-November 1954, were only to remain in original form for four years, as they were rebuilt by the operator to front-entrance full-fronted form between November 1958 and March 1960.

The last L-type bus bodies to the traditional half-cab design (8427-32) were built in 1955 for Western National and Southern National, each taking three 30ft by 7ft 6in 39-seat bodies on Bristol L5G chassis dating from the 1938-42 period, lengthened and updated to 'LL' specification. The Western National buses were from that company's own fleet, but the Southern National ones, all dating from 1939, had begun life with Eastern Counties, later being purchased by SN after a brief period with Lincolnshire in 1954. Numerically the last, with body 8432, was 379 (CVF 854) seen here.

for Pat Hearn Ltd but were taken over by Tilling in 1951. The new bodies were to a modified version of the 1951 design but 28ft. 10in. long, having a revised grille design and with a two-and-one seating layout for 24 passengers for London sightseeing tour duties – they re-entered service in July 1957.

The position with regard to 'old-generation' double-deck bodywork was different, with a much stronger continuity of new construction. The highbridge body on Bristol KSW6B or KSW6G chassis was still favoured by the Bristol and the Brighton Hove & District fleets, batches for both being included in the 1955, 1956 and 1957 programmes, together adding up to 147 buses. This was an indication of the regard for the model in those fleets, though another factor at Brighton was a need for 7ft. 6in. buses, of which batches were built for BH&D in 1955 and 1957.

The Bristol operating and vehicle-constructing companies had become separate by this date, Bristol Commercial Vehicles Ltd becoming operational on 1st January 1955 (whilst the company had been registered as long ago as 1943, it had not been activated). The

realities of the activities of the operating company were recognised when the old title of the Bristol Tramways & Carriage Co Ltd was changed to the Bristol Omnibus Co Ltd on 16th May 1957. It was the latter that received the last K-type bodies when the final two of the last batch of 27 for Bristol (9630-56) were delivered to the operator on 14th September 1957.

Rebodying of double-deckers for various Tilling and Scottish group companies had continued intermittently, designs varying to suit the dimensional requirements of the different types of chassis, as shown in accompanying illustrations. This was, however, on a much smaller scale than in earlier years, ending with the 1955 programme year. Indeed, from then onwards, rebodying became more a matter of occasional replacement of bodywork that had suffered severe fire or accident damage than the extended use of sound chassis that had been common practice previously. This was partly because older types of vehicle were being judged unsuitable in relation to their design or dimensions, and also because ECW's aluminium-alloy bodywork was proving to have durability which was comparable to the chassis.

The 60-seat highbridge Bristol KSW continued to have quite a strong following. In the 1954 programme, 106 were built in batches 156-8 between June of that year and the following February. Generally the design was unchanged, but fifteen for Brighton Hove & District (7247-61) introduced a feature that was to continue for some time as an exclusive BH&D characteristic. This was the provision of a continuous metal louvre above all side windows on each deck. This had been quite a common practice, sometimes shaped to follow the window outline at the ends, but was last seen on ECW bodywork in 1940. In the BH&D case, no attempt at shaping was made, giving rather an austere look, and it was coupled with the use of the Beatonson Rapide sliding and tipping window in alternate bays. The main KSW highbridge customer that year was Bristol Tramways, with 71 (7383-450 and 7799/800 plus 7382 for Cheltenham District, now under its wing), split between KSW6B and KSW6G, but United, once a lowbridge stronghold, took 20 KSW6B (body numbers 7451-65 and 7600-4).

By 1955, output of the Lodekka LD type was growing rapidly, that year's programme total of 329 being not only about double the previous year's figure but outnumbering all the company's other products put together. The main 1954 programme LD batches were 151-5, though there was the usual spill-over effect, with some in batch 133 and others in 170 and 179. The main 1955 programme batches for this model were 170-6, with some bodies in 153/4 and 183-5. Few changes other than variations to suit individual operators' needs were found necessary. The most obvious in this period was the introduction of the shorter radiator grille which responded to a general trend in motor vehicle styling but seemed particularly effective in the case of the Lodekka, giving a more balanced look. It came into effect after about May 1955, on the later vehicles in the 1954 programme and, in addition, from batch 154 at about the same time, the standard seating capacity went up from 58 to 60, a design modification having allowed two more in the lower deck. The option of platform doors was common but by no means universal and another variant arose where operators did not require doors but wanted the capabilty to fit them later – ultimately some seven platform design variants for the LD were recorded. This official view shows West Yorkshire DX34 (OWX 178), an LD6B with platform doors, one of 25, and in this case (body 8133) built in batch 175, catching the winter sunshine before delivery early in 1956. It had platform design No. 3, widely used where doors were specified – the variations are explained in Appendix 3.

Production of LS single-deckers was generally straightforward, the 1954 programme including 156 buses (7478-519, 7629-98, 7704-21/31-55/808) in batches 141 and 159-64, except for five unbatched. Two of these, 7808, an LS5G for Lincolnshire, shown here, and 7498, one of the uncommon LS6B, for United Welsh, were high-capacity buses seating 54, this being acheived by adopting 'three and two' seating, just possible with legal minimum seat width within the 8ft overall width. Satisfactory emergency exit access was clearly a problem, so this was moved to a centre rear position. The idea was not found acceptable and was not repeated. Also unbatched were three more two-door saloons for United Counties. There were also 25 express bodies (7520-44) in batch 165, 20 going to West Yorkshire and five to United Counties.

By 1955, the express version of the LS had taken on a little more of the style of its L-type predecessor, with the adoption of the stepped waistband. This picture of West Yorkshire EUG29 (OWX141), one of a further 20 LS5G for this operator, also shows a detail modification which had been introduced near the end of the 1954 programme. This was the increased rake applied to the upper part of the windscreen, giving an effect not unlike that on one of the prototypes in this respect – it seems probable that this was done to reduce reflections from the interior at night. The 1955 programme included 61 buses for Tilling companies (8144-99 and 8392-6) in batches 161, 163 and 164, plus 38 express versions (8200-34/44-6) in batch 178, the vehicle illustrated having body 8215, delivered in April 1955.

The interior of the LS express body offered quite a high standard of comfort, with a type of seat very similar not only to those in the L-type express body but also those in North Western's pre-war saloons, which were virtually to coach standards of comfort. The overall effect, if not lavish, was quite attractive and well suited to medium-distance express-service duty. The photograph shows the West Yorkshire vehicle illustrated above, but the design, generally with green moquette, was standard in most Tilling fleets using such vehicles.

An unexpected outlet for what was virtually the standard highbridge 27ft. by 8ft. body, as built on Bristol KSW chassis, came when an order for five examples (10004-8) based on Leyland Titan PD2/20 concealed radiator chassis was placed by Sheffield Joint Omnibus Committee. This was possible because Sheffield was one of four municipalities which had entered into agreements with railway companies under which part or all of the local services, though run by buses managed by the transport department of the municipality, were administered by a joint committee involving the railways. The crucial point which allowed the purchase of ECW bodywork at that period was that some of the buses were owned directly by the British Railways Board, whose name appeared on the side as legal owner even though the vehicles were in municipal livery. The five vehicles were delivered in June 1957, two going to Sheffield's 'C' fleet (all of which were railway-owned) and three to the 'B' fleet, forming part of

the railway share of that section of the fleet, which included both municipal and railway-owned buses, sharing the working of specified routes. A similar small delivery of single-deck vehicles followed two years later, but otherwise this opening for wider use of ECW bodywork was not pursued further.

Much more significant was the opening up of orders from the Scottish group companies within the BTC empire. The group continued to follow a policy of purchasing its vehicles from various sources, but from the spring of 1954, sizeable batches of Bristol-ECW vehicles began to be included in its intake of new vehicles. The first to arrive in March and April 1954 were 30 LS6G coaches for Scottish Omnibuses, of which the bodies (7769-98) were based on the standard ECW design of the time, but with a 38-seat capacity and having various minor differences in trim. In the 1955 programme, 25 Lodekka LD6G were supplied to Central SMT and 20 to Western SMT as well

Bristol-ECW vehicles made their first appearance in a Scottish Bus Group fleet in March-April 1954, when Scottish Omnibuses took delivery of 30 LS6G coaches (7769-98, not batched). Though basically to standard design, they had several special features, including an inward-opening entrance door, 38-seat capacity and two destination screens below the windscreen, allowing the addition of glazed panels in the front roof dome as well as the more usual cantrail windows. At that date SOL was still using the SMT diamond emblem and this was carried on the front between the headlamps. A further 53 LS coaches were built in that year's programme for Tilling companies (7545-89, 7626-8 and 7764-68, in batches 147-9), all completed by the end of June that year. Most were to the standard pattern, though ten for United had a similar destination display to the SOL examples and other features similar to the earlier Royal Tiger batches.

Only one batch of LS models with bus bodywork was supplied to the Scottish Bus Group, these being 20 (8293-8312) for W. Alexander & Sons Ltd, built in batch 180 and delivered in February-March 1955. They were basically standard, but had a shallow single-line destination display with three-track number built into one end which fitted neatly into the front dome outline. Various other features, including the type of seats and exterior trim details, conformed to SBG practice. Some, at least, were in cream and blue Bluebird livery at first, but E14 (FWG 849), with body 8306, was in blue and cream when seen at Kirkaldy in April 1960.

The 1955 programme included Lodekka deliveries for Scottish fleets for the first time, and Central SMT B10 (GM 7010) with body 8292 was one of an initial order for 25 LD6G for this fleet. It was produced as part of batch 179 and delivered sufficiently early in 1955 to have the early production long radiator grille. Also evident in this view is the two-aperture front destination display used on these vehicles and 20 for Western SMT.

as 20 LS6G buses for Alexander. In subsequent years the LD6G was supplied to Scottish companies in large numbers and indeed later types of Lodekka were to remain in favour for as long as they were available.

Another family of body design was founded in 1954 as a result of the introduction of the Bristol SC. The increase in maximum dimensions had revealed that there was a continuing need for a 35-seat bus, particularly for use in rural areas, where falling passenger traffic made economy of operation essential. The design had to be capable of driver-only operation (also soon to come into favour in some fleets on the LS saloon types) and provide exceptional fuel economy. Bristol produced a chassis of conventional front-engined layout using proprietary components such as axles and brake system from the contemporary Bedford SB. The two prototypes SCX.001 and 002 had, respectively, a Gardner 4LK and a Perkins P6 engine, though the latter choice was not repeated. The bodywork (7801-2) was of full-fronted type, construction of the whole vehicle being designed to save weight – unladen weight of the first prototype was 3 tons 18cwt. External appearance was neat, set off by a miniature version of the Bristol grille on

The first Bristol SC ('small capacity') prototype, chassis SCX.001 with Gardner 4LK engine, photographed after completion as Eastern National 395 (724 APU), with body 7801 and ready for delivery in October 1954. It was used by Bristol and toured various operators before entering normal service. The Bedford origin of the axles is readily deduced from the chromium-plated hub cap, as found on contemporary Bedford SB models.

Production of the SC got under way as part of the 1955 programme, the first deliveries beginning in February 1956. Seen here is one of the first order for Lincolnshire, 2410 in that fleet (NFW 651) with body 8374 in course of delivery in May of that year. That fleet was to receive 34 (8365-86, 8451-62) but 8459 was diverted to Crosville. The largest batch in that year's deliveries went to Eastern Counties, however, which got 37 (8313-49), these being equipped from the start for one-man operation, as it was always called in those days.

(Below) The use of a single rear window with quite broad corner panels gave the SC a rear-end appearance rather reminiscent of much older designs. Seen here is the third prototype, SCX.003, after delivery to Eastern Counties as LC501 (TVF 501). This had body 7625, and differed from the previous two in having more opening windows and other less noticeable details.

the front panel. The first vehicle was delivered initially to Bristol on 27th October 1954, though both were for the Eastern National fleet, in which they were numbered 395 and 396, the second going there direct a month later.

A third prototype, SCX.003, with body 7625, was delivered to Bristol in shell form in October 1955 before being completed for Eastern Counties in December of that year. By then regular production was beginning, the first deliveries going to Eastern Counties with 37 examples (8313-49), equipped from new for driver-only operation. Lincolnshire were to have 35 (8365-86 and 8451-62) but one (8459) was diverted to Crosville. All three companies

were subsequently to build up sizeable fleets of the type over the next five years or so. The Gardner 4LK engine, of a mere 3.8 litres, gave only modest performance and, with the unglazed internal bulkhead, considerable internal noise, but fuel consumption figures of 20 miles per gallon could be achieved on suitable routes.

A project which never got beyond the stage of a single prototype so far as ECW was concerned again involved London Transport. The first two prototype Routemaster integral-construction double-deckers had been built at LT's Chiswick works in 1954-55 with close involvement from AEC in terms of mechanical units and Park Royal in regard to body construction. It was expected at that stage that the numbers of buses of this type needed would be comparable to that for the RT family, of which 6,956 had been built for London Transport and of which 2,131 had been supplied on Leyland chassis derived from the PD2 but extensively modified to conform to the RT specification and classified by LTE as their RTL and RTW chassis, with 1,631 and 500 examples respectively. There were two main body suppliers, Park Royal and Weymann, as well as several smaller quantities from other concerns. London Transport wished to avoid being in the hands of a monopoly supplier (AEC and Park Royal being associated companies) and it was agreed that two further Routemaster prototypes

Very much a one-off, the prototype Green Line coach version of the Routemaster was intended as part of an exercise to widen London Transport's sources of supply when this new integral design went into production, not pursued in the event. ECW was given the task of building this last of the four Routemaster prototypes, based on the LT/Park Royal design, using running gear from Leyland. It was allocated the ECW number 8250 and the fact that 8251 was not issued suggests that originally there may have been the possibility of another. Inevitably, the appearance was pure RM, although this vehicle originally had the rather unsatisfactory 'interim' grille and bonnet shown, which had resulted from a redesign of the front end during the development of the first two vehicles. The vehicle had been given the fleet number CRL4 when new in February 1957 but had become RMC4 to conform to the production Routemaster coaches by then in service when this photograph was taken in Harlow in April 1963. In later years it received new front panels, with four headlamps and other details conforming to the RMC pattern.

would be built, one at Weymann and one at Eastern Coach Works, both to have Leyland mechanical units. The ECW vehicle, given the body number 8250, was to be a Green Line coach, with 57 seats rather than the 64 of the bus version.

The set of running units were received from Leyland on 9th February 1955 but it was not until 22nd February 1957 that the completed vehicle, numbered CRL4 by LTE was delivered. The body design was virtually identical to the Park Royal version, and therefore structurally as well as visually very different to any other ECW product, even though the firm was by then well used to its own forms of integral construction with the LS and, in regard to integrated design, the Lodekka. It was built to drawings prepared by LTE/PRV/AEC as far as the basic design and appearance

of the body was concerned but in conjunction with ECW engineers, minor points of ECW constructional practice being included. Many modifications were incorporated as the work progressed, almost inevitable in a development vehicle of such advanced design, but even before it was delivered it had become clear that the numbers required would not make it economic to build at more than one concern and the first bulk order for 650 buses was placed with Park Royal in October 1956, even though production did not begin until two years later. Thus CRL4 was destined to remain unique even before it was completed – it entered service on 9th October 1957.

The Routemaster had not been the first ECW product to wear Green Line livery. In 1953, experimental running of three lightweight single-deckers was carried out, as it was thought that there would be a need for extra vehicles beyond the new fleet of 263 RF-type AEC Regal IV coaches with Metro-Cammell bodywork. London Transport had placed great importance to keeping weight down, a subject of renewed interest at the time, and the RF, though very satisfactory in most respects, was heavier than the corresponding RT double-decker. An LS5G with virtually standard ECW 45-seat bus body, 6110, included in batch 118, was delivered in February as a Bristol Tramways vehicle but with Green Line insignia, spending some time working on Green Line route 711 and on local routes from Reigate garage alongside a Leyland Tiger Cub and an AEC Monocoach. Here also, shrinking needs resulted in no order being placed, though it must be said that the lack of any concession to London Transport's ideas in specification suggests that expectations of an order were not high. The LS5G, Bristol 2828 (PHW 918), is seen in Regent Street in company with an RT in June 1953, decorations for the Coronation being in evidence in the background.

A revised design for the Lodekka LD body, referred to internally as the Mark 2, first appeared on a single prototype (8010), built on an LD5G for Eastern National, in whose fleet it was 1485 (433 FEV). It was built in the 1955 programme as one of the vehicles in batch 175, and delivered on 20th January 1956. The most obvious change was the sloping of the underside of the canopy and of the corresponding top edge of the cab side windows, but there was another change to the lower edge of the cab door window, now horizontal again, though raised above the level of the main waistline. The upper edge of the front bulkhead windows also became horizontal. These modifications were adopted as standard part-way through the 1956 programme of 377 LD bodies, the change appearing at the beginning of batch 185 and the first examples going out to Crosville and United Counties on 29th June 1956.

An important option taken up in a big way by Tilling companies was the Cave-Browne-Cave heating and ventilating system developed by a Southampton University professor of that name. In essence, the conventional radiator's function, plus that of heater units, was taken over by two units mounted each side of the front destination box, feeding air to both decks, heated as desired, as well as cooling the engine. The two first Lodekka installations were in Mark 1 vehicles delivered in May 1956, initially to Bristol; Cumberland 369 (RAO 733), an LD6G with body 8540, shown here in Carlisle (by then renumbered 416) in July 1962, and United BL6 (106 BHN), an LD6B with body 8619. Two more in Mark 2 bodies 8557, and 8587, repectively Eastern National 1489, an LD5G, and Hants & Dorset 1367, an LD6B, followed in October. The front openings and exit vanes on each side were readily identifiable: the normal hinged vents above the front upper-deck windows were omitted, though a small ventilator intake was added above the centre pillar. The 'broken' upper-deck waistband was soon to become a common feature.

Output of LS models continued through the 1956 programme and into that for 1957 without significant change to the basic bus and express designs. The 1956 programme included 139 buses and 43 express versions built in batches 191 (mainly express) and 195-7, though thirteen were unbatched. Body numbers were 8736-63/76-83, 8834-934/8/9/41-55, 9040-57). The 1957 programme was complicated in terms of body numbers by the introduction of the MW, described in the next chapter, but a further 73 buses, with various numbers between 9659 and 9868, were built in batches 205/6, plus five two-door buses for Hants & Dorset (there had also been seven in the previous year's total) unbatched, and 18 express (9884-9900 plus one replacement body, 9698, for Crosville, on a 1952 underframe) in batch 204. All these LS vehicles were delivered by the end of 1957. The United express example shown in London, BUE11 (311 FHN), with body 9884, one of five on the comparatively rare LS6B chassis and showing another livery variant, was among these. United also had some 269 LS5G buses by this time.

95

In 1957, the advent of second-generation new models was accompanied by final manifestations of older designs, sometimes in new forms. The 'Queen Mary' coach body had gone out of general production after 26 were built in 1952 (6261-86), in which a final batch of ten LWL6B coaches had gone to Bristol, plus ten on LL and six on rebuilt Regals for Tilling. The appearance of more examples to basically similar outline five years later came as quite a surprise. United had been operating a batch of special centre-entrance single-deckers on the Scarborough sea-front service since 1935, transferring the original bodies, built by the local Plaxton concern on 1928 ADC chassis, to 1938 Leyland Tiger in 1950, but now a fresh start was made. Ten Bristol L5G chassis of 1946/7 were lengthened to 30ft and new ECW bodies 9993-10002 built, using the 'Queen Mary' structure but modified to centre-entrance layout and having the main destination display also positioned centrally over the entrance and on the opposite side, with only one small box at the front. Inside, 39 bus seats were provided, but with generous roof glazing. The last of the batch, BGS10 (998 CHN) is shown in service.

The London-based Tilling coach fleet also came back for five more bodies (10012-6) of a design derived from the same origin. This time, AEC Regal III preselective gearbox models dating from 1949 that had been taken over with the business of P. Hearn were concerned, the original Strachans bodywork being replaced by a 28ft 10in by 7ft 6in 24-seat touring-coach version of the 'Queen Mary', but with several differences. There was a new type of grille, similar to, though larger than, those on SC-type coaches also being completed about the same time, July 1957. The sweep-down of the waistline into the front corners was less pronounced and the external trim was altered in style. Seen here in the picturesque village of Dunster in Devon in May 1958 is KLA 90, with body 10013.

The Bristol K-series finally came to the end of production in 1957. There had been 65 KSW, all bodied as 60-seat highbridge, in the 1955 programme (7809-73), built in 1955-6, 40 programmed and built in 1956 (8686-8725) and a further 27 (9630-56) in 1957. The 1955-6 deliveries had been split between Bristol Tramways (including some for its subsidiaries) and Brighton Hove & District. The 1957 examples on KSW-type chassis were all for Bristol (see the facing page), though the company's name changed to Bristol Omnibus part-way through the contract. Brighton Hove & District also had a final batch of eight (9603-10), but these were 7ft 6in-wide on KS6G chassis, specially ordered for busy routes 3 and 3A which ran through some narrow streets – they were also noteworthy as seating 62, with an extra pair at the extreme rear of the upper deck, the gangway being extended to allow this. There was a slight difference in the application of the beading on the cab front, fitted in KSW rather than previous KS style – perhaps the latter had been forgotten since the previous examples were built. Seen here in the town centre is 497 (HPM 497) with body 9607.

Appropriately, it was the Bristol undertaking itself which received the last Bristol K-series buses to enter service, which were also the last chassis to receive this style of body from ECW. They had bodies 9655/6 on the Bristol Omnibus Co Ltd's C8430/1 (YHT 926/7), both KSW6G, delivered from Lowestoft on 14th September 1957. The second of these is seen here after arrival, in company with the first K-type, Bristol's C3082 (EAE 280) with K5G chassis 42.1. built in 1937, with the Bristol-built 56-seat body it had carried since 1949, when it had also received the usual PV2 radiator fitted to vehicles rebodied. Despite the Lodekka chassis with all its implications on British bus design being a Bristol product, the 'home' company had continued to favour the K-series for much of its needs, building up a fleet of 353 highbridge KSW, or in a few cases KS with 8ft. bodywork, since 1951.

Chapter Five: **A second generation**

As described in the previous chapter, by the mid-'fifties Bristol and ECW had become closely linked in the production of both single- and double-deck buses which incorporated advanced design principles. Despite the assured need for their output from the Tilling and other BTC operating companies, there was no sense of complacency and the existing models were under constant review to see if changes should be introduced. This applied to both minor details as well as to the completely revised versions of the basic types.

The MW single-deckers

The LS semi-integral single-decker had proved quite successful but the general interest of the British bus industry in such lines of development had not materialised in the way that had been expected. Other manufacturers' integral models had not gained widespread favour – neither Leyland's co-operation with MCW, nor AEC's with Park Royal, in the manufacture of integral or semi-integral single-deckers had attracted many orders from

The introduction of the MW was conducted in a very low-key fashion, with barely any publicity. Eastern National 434 (1858 F), was one of the three prototypes to receive saloon bodywork, this one being 9736. It was an MW5G and had the high-level radiator used with the optional Cave-Browne-Cave heating system. The lines of the MW body were a curious mixture of more rounded contours at the front and an unusually upright rear profile.

If anything, the upright look of the express version of the body for the MW chassis was more noticeable than that of the bus, for although the latter's near-vertical profile extended higher, the destination display made it seem more logical. On the express version, the rear window was rather taller, and setting it almost vertical gave an effect reminiscent of designs of a much earlier period, perhaps going back to the late 'twenties. The example shown was the only express body built as one of the set of seven prototype vehicles, 9901, on West Yorkshire EUG70 (TWT 122), an MW5G, delivered in the latter part of 1957.

British operators. The growing interest in relatively light or medium-weight vehicles had resulted in many companies outside the Tilling Group adopting models such as the Leyland Tiger Cub or AEC Reliance. However, it had become evident that careful choice of design throughout the vehicle could virtually match the weight-saving that had been associated with the integral, but retaining the simpler manufacturing process of the separate chassis and body.

It was therefore decided to follow a similar philosophy in a replacement for the LS. This was the Bristol MW, which reverted to a conventional chassis frame, but otherwise retained much of the mechanical design of the LS, with similar options of engine – production vehicles being of MW5G or MW6G type, with Gardner 5HLW or 6HLW horizontal engines, as used in most LS vehicles. The frame design had conventional pressed-steel sidemembers, with a shape which was generally straight but was cranked so as to be at a raised height over the amidships engine location. This left ECW free to construct an aluminium alloy floor frame and although this was additional to the chassis, the latter's simplicity and the choice of materials caused the weight difference to be

quite slight. Typically, MW saloons weighed about 6.5 tons and MW coaches around 7 tons, rarely averaging more than about 3cwt above LS equivalents, though specifications and individual vehicles could vary.

Seven pre-production chassis were built in 1957, numbered 135.001-007, and ECW built bodies for them, comprising three stage carriage bus bodies, one 'express', two coaches and an incomplete shell. The last, initially having a Bristol engine, was sent to Bristol for use as a test and development vehicle, although most of the others of this batch were also sent there initially before delivery to the operator.

There were strong similarities between the MW and the LS, but the bus and express versions in particular were altered quite significantly at front and rear. At the front, the previous rather upright effect, with recessed windscreens, gave way to a design with more of a curved profile from the waist level upwards. It could be described as not unlike that of the coach version, save that the windscreen continued to be set lower than the side windows so that there was room for the comparatively deep destination display. The top of the front panel of the

The characteristic frontal appearance of the MW stage carriage body was 'softer' than the LS, with more than a hint of the contemporary ECW coach about it. Production got under way promptly after the ending of LS output, the 1957 programme total of 108 bus bodies built in batches 208-210 beginning delivery on the last day of that year, with three vehicles for Red & White and one for United. This one for Red & White, with body 9755, came early in 1958, even though identified as a 1957 bus by the last two figures of its fleet number, U957, under that operator's system. It was one of 37 MW6G buses, all 45-seat, added to the fleet under the 1957 programme, beginning with one of the prototypes.

The express version of the MW had a little less of the 'dolled-up bus' about it than the LS, and could look quite smart, at least from a view that did not reveal the upright rear end of early examples. Midland General had a long tradition of vehicles of such character, not necessarily for long-distance services, going back to Weymann-bodied AEC Regals of the 'thirties, and had its own ideas on the use of polished aluminium external trim. Seen here is one of ten MW6G with 43-seat bodywork built in February to July 1958 and forming part of ECW's 1957 programme total of 26 MW express bodies produced in batch 207. Mount Street, Nottingham, is the location of this view of 256 (25 DRB) with body 9876, seen with various vehicles of Barton Transport.

folding entrance door was shaped to match this profile. At the rear, the MW bus and express versions were, by contrast, more upright in outline than the LS. Rounded ends to the divided rear window gave an effect like two facing segments.

The coach design, on the other hand, was almost unchanged in outline, though the addition of a low-set radiator grille distinguished the MW from the previous LS. This was because the new chassis had the radiator at the front instead of being set back behind the front axle, as had been the case on the LS, where it drew air from underneath the front panels. However, there was growing interest in improved heating systems at this time, and the Tilling companies took up the work of Professor Cave-Brown-Cave, who devised an arrangement in which the conventional radiator was replaced by what amounted to a dual-purpose system which combined engine cooling and saloon heating. The single-deck version of this had a broader but much shallower rectangular grille divided in the centre mounted only a little way below windscreen level and replacing the winged motif which contained an intake for the previous type of heater. Its introduction as an option virtually coincided with the appearance of the MW prototypes, though it did also appear on some late LS models.

The pre-production MW chassis were given bodies bearing numbers related to the operating companies' orders then in hand. Thus the three buses were for Eastern National (9736), Red & White (9747) and United (9819), the express vehicle for West Yorkshire (9901) and the two coaches for Crosville (8433) and Eastern National (9915). The shell body for use by Bristol Commercial Vehicles was 9697. The first to be delivered left the works on 2nd July 1957, this being the Red & White bus, an MW6G, on numerically the last of these chassis, 135.007. Conversely, numerically the first body (8433), the Crosville coach, was not delivered until April 1958, well after production deliveries had begun.

Manufacture of production LS bus and express versions ended by the end of 1957 and the production changeover to the new model virtually coincided with the new year, the first four, three MW6G buses for Red & White and one MW5G bus for United being delivered on 31st December 1957. The coach version came a little later, in February 1958, following closely behind the pre-production versions in this case. The first production MW coaches to be delivered, on 21st February 1958, were the initial three (10017-19) of a batch of 20 MW6G for Scottish Omnibuses, in whose fleet they were A622-624, though followed closely by deliveries of the first Royal Blue (Southern and Western National) examples. There was a slight overlap in a sense, for United, somewhat surprisingly, reverted to the LS coach for its 1958 order for five vehicles which were built on the last LS underframes to be built, 119.201-205, and had body numbers 10656-60 – they were delivered in April and May 1958 and had a 34-seat capacity for touring duties.

Overall, however, there was a straightforward transition from the LS to the MW. The latter was hardly publicised at all in the technical press but production continued steadily into the early 'sixties and, although reduced by the arrival on the scene of the RE rear-engined model, continued on a limited scale until 1967. The total of MW-type bodies built by ECW over that period was 1,913 compared to 1,392 LS, the individual figures (LS in brackets) for the various types being 1,095 (777) bus, 234 (194) express, and 584 (421) coach, though the last comparison is complicated by a major body design change in 1961 to which reference will be made later. Taken together, the total of roundly 3,000 vehicles, almost two-thirds of them buses, made a significant contribution to the transport scene of the time, familiar in most parts of England and Wales though to a much more limited extent in Scotland.

Closely related to the MW coach design of the period were two instances of orders for coaches built by ECW on

The close relationship between the standard coach body as built in its final form for the LS and the initial version for the MW is conveyed by these two views of Royal Blue examples, in both cases owned by Western National. The upper photograph, taken at Victoria in September 1958, shows 2205 (VDV 748), an LS6G with body 9966, built as part of the 1957 programme of 49 coaches, all in batch 203, for various Tilling companies and delivered between February and July that year. There had been no design changes of any significance apart from those for individual companies since 1954, although the numbers built in the meantime had been modest – eighteen in batch 177 in 1955 and 38 in batch 190 in 1956. The 1957 Royal Blue orders, six each for Western and Southern National, were the first without the roof-mounted luggage carrier, and the dark blue and cream livery had been simplified, though still very effective.

The lower view shows 2238 (XUO 721), an MW6G with body 10047, one of the 102 MW coaches for Tilling and Scottish companies in the 1958 programme, again delivered in the February-July period. The most obvious new feature was the rectangular radiator grille mounted low down on the front panel. The inward-opening door was now standard and, at the rear, the panels below the waist were now vertical instead of having a slight curve. There was some evidence of a general policy of simplification of specifications, with less brightwork, as evident here, though such matters depended to some degree on operators' requirements.

The curved-profile coach design had a long run with no more than minor changes to the basic design. Production quantities varied – the 1959 programme was fairly small at 55 MW examples in batches 243 and 244, for example. The figure fell further to 45 for 1960, in batches 267 and 268, but in addition, five unbatched bodies (12067-71) were built on the five AEC Regal IV chassis dating from 1951 operated by Tilling Transport which originally had 'Continental' bodies similar to the London Transport RFW batch. The new body suited them well, the opportunity being taken to incorporate some of the options quite widely taken up by other operators such as the positioning of the destination boxes below the windscreen. The body design required little adaptation for the Regal IV chassis, even an MW-like though smaller grille being incorporated to improve air flow to the set-back radiator, and the winged emblem above it carried TT lettering in place of the Bristol-ECW badge. Seen here in Edinburgh on tour for Thomas Cook, then also part of the BTC organisation, is LYM 731, with body 12067.

Sheffield was the only municipal undertaking with which ECW did any business during the years of complete State ownership, once the outstanding order for Middlesbrough had been completed in 1950. This was possible because parts of the municipally-managed fleet were railway-owned, which meant that they were part of the British Transport Commission's domain and ECW could trade with them. Sheffield Joint Omnibus Committee ordered five Leyland Titan PD2/20 chassis with ECW 59-seat highbridge bodywork (10004-8) which were delivered in June 1957. At that date, the last bodies on Bristol KSW chassis were in hand, and the Sheffield bodies were based on the style being built for that model, though the full-width bonnet and concealed radiator on that version of the PD2 made the overall effect very different, especially with Sheffield's cream and blue livery. The order represented only a small part of the undertaking's new vehicle intake, for which such firms as Weymann or Roe generally provided the bodywork. Seen here in the Pond Street bus station is 1294 (YWB 294) with body 10008, parked in front of a 1948 AEC Regent III with Roberts bodywork.

non-Bristol chassis. In 1960. the five AEC Regal IV coaches dating from 1951 operated by Tillings Transport (BTC) Ltd, originally fitted with ECW bodies of similar design to the fifteen best known as the London Transport RFW class, were given new ECW bodies (12067-71) to a style almost identical to the contemporary standard, though with the front axle set back slightly more than the MW, with benefit to the entrance design, and the fuel filler was on the nearside rather than the offside. The original bodies were sold to a dealer and at least one found further use on another chassis.

Sheffield Joint Omnibus Committee decided upon the Leyland chassis plus ECW body combination for a second occasion in 1961, this time choosing the Leopard underfloor-engined chassis and single-deck bodywork to coach standards. Here again, there were slight changes to the design to suit the chassis, this being of the L1 type as originally produced when the Leopard was introduced in 1959 as a 30ft. model with chassis design very similar to the Tiger Cub lightweight model but with the larger O.600 9.8-litre engine. The body design also incorporated other features to suit the customer, such as the use of polished

Four years went by, during which no Sheffield Joint Omnibus Committee orders arrived at Lowestoft, and then one for five coach bodies on Leyland Leopard L1 chassis was received, for use on some of the undertaking's longer routes. The standard coach design was modified to suit and the result was functional yet attractive, as can be judged from this view of 1182 (1882 WA) with body 12257. The letter C above the fleet number signifies that it belonged to the 'C' fleet, owned entirely by British Railways.

Most of the SC models were buses but a coach version first appeared, unbatched, as part of the 1956 programme. The seven coach bodies built (9192-9), for Eastern Counties, were delivered in June of that year whereas the 57 SC buses (8956-9012) built in batches 194, 211 and 212, did not begin to come through until November, continuing right through 1957 and into early 1958. The differences were largely cosmetic, and even the 33 seats were of semi-coach type though a luggage boot was included at the rear. Apart from coach livery, with appropriate brightwork and a sliding door, perhaps the most striking change was the replacement of the usual radiator grille by a recessed opening, giving an effect a little like that of the contemporary Triumph TR2 sports car. Seen in Nottingham when only a few weeks old is LSC872 (TVF 872) with body 9198.

The following year, another small batch of thirteen SC coaches (9970-82) appeared, three more for Eastern Counties, this time with 35 seats, and ten 33-seat versions for Lincolnshire. Much of the design continued, but the grille was changed to the more ornate version shown, which was to recur in much the same form on various full-fronted single-deck body designs for front-engined chassis over the next few years. Lincolnshire 2604 (OFW 801) with body 9976 is also seen in Nottingham in July 1957. Note that both this and the vehicle shown above have windscreen wiper blades out of position, off the screen, suggesting either an over-zealous cleaner or some problem with the mechanism. The same pattern of construction applied with the 42 buses in the 1957 programme in batches 194, 211 and 212 not delivered until later that year and into 1958.

mouldings above and below the dark blue waistband forming part of the Sheffield livery, the basic colour being cream. Instead of the downward curve of the waist on the cab side and passenger entry door there was a stepped break in the window line, though the windscreen and general design of the front end, including the grille, was largely of MW style.

The Sheffield vehicles had separate route number and destination displays in a box with the face slightly more upright than, for example, the Crosville MW coach style of the time. They were intended largely for use on some of the medium-distance services operated by that undertaking, the 41-seat bodywork offering a high standard of comfort – two were for the 'B' fleet and three for the 'C' fleet. Allocated body numbers 12255-59 following on from the 1961 Tilling coach programme vehicles, they were delivered between 24th March and 20th April 1961.

The demand for a smaller and lighter type of single-decker was being met by the Bristol SC type, as described in the previous chapter, but the body design developed for it was also used for rebodying Bristol L-type and other chassis in a way which made them suitable for one-person operation. The forward-entrance layout and full-fronted cab suited this requirement, and the body design could be lengthened if need be. Some of the Tilling companies had coaches of which the half-cab bodywork had become outdated and in some cases the body framing was subject

to the wood-rot problem common on early post-war vehicles, quite apart from being unsuited for stage carriage duties. The chassis were still in good order, however, and the largest programme of this kind was carried out for the Southern National and Western National companies, for whom twelve (10720-31) and fourteen (10738-51) bodies were built on L-type chassis which had carried Beadle coach bodywork for use on Royal Blue services, but extended to 30ft. form and reclassified LL. Six similar 39-seat bodies (10732-7) were built for Thames Valley, again on lengthened L-type chassis in this case previously fitted with Vincent or Windover coach bodywork. All 32 were delivered between May and September 1958. A similar body but of 27ft. 6in. length was completed in December that year on a Leyland PS1 chassis for the Cumberland fleet (10633), again replacing a coach body, in that case by ACB (Associated Coachbuilders of Sunderland). All of these vehicles had a slightly bulbous front panel with a style of grille having a broad panel with fine vertical bars superimposed on a narrower one with horizontal bars introduced for the 1957 33-seat coach version of the SC model, the bus version continuing with the small Bristol-style grille.

Similar bodywork was also built for rebodying former Bristol L-type coaches in Tilling fleets during 1959-62 – four more for Thames Valley in 1959, eighteen for Hants & Dorset at the rate of six per year in 1960-62. In addition

The SC body design provided a basis for rebodying sound Bristol L-type chassis, of which several fleets had a surplus as a result of changes in coach fashion, as buses for operation without conductors. Some 26 former Royal Blue coaches were handled in this way, the chassis being lengthened to LL specification and the body built to 30ft. overall length to accommodate 39 passengers. The L-type radiator was accommodated by using a front panel giving a step in the profile and the grille was the 'SC coach' type rather than something more akin to the Lodekka, as might have been expected. Like all but one of the ex-Royal Blue vehicles, Western National 1202 (JUO 934), with new body 10739, was an L6B, effectively becoming LL6B. Note the way in which the offside emergency exit door split the bay rearwards of the rear axle.

The rebodying of Bristol L-type chassis to this pattern continued on a modest scale until 1962. Hants & Dorset 677 (KEL 405) was one of six rebodied for this fleet in 1961 – it had started life as an L6G coach but was re-engined with a Bristol AVW unit as well as lengthened to receive body 12780. The SC ancestry of the design is obvious from this view and the overall effect had lost the character – some might say the styling triumph – of the original L-type bus body of 1946-52. Note the prominent reversing lamp, essential if the driver was to cope with such manoeuvres unaided at night.

Southern Vectis replaced the standard 35-seat ECW saloon bodies on three L-type buses of 1946 in 1961-62 but in this case the chassis were not lengthened. Further vehicles were rebuilt by operators in their own workshops in various ways – Cumberland built its own bodywork for ten more PS1 chassis to a simpler design, retaining the half-cab layout – while mention should be made at this point of Wilts & Dorset's rebuilding of the ECW bodies of its fifteen 'late' LWL5G models of 1954 with a full-width cab, giving a somewhat similar appearance, though with a different radiator cowl and grille design, between November 1958 and March 1960.

The Railbuses

British Railways undertook a large-scale conversion from steam to diesel motive power in the 'fifties. The diesel railcar became a familiar sight, most of the big fleet placed in service being of a relatively heavy-duty type mounted on bogies and intended to operate in two-car or larger sets. They were built by various concerns largely with railway-carriage building experience even though most of the underframes came from British United Traction, a joint AEC and Leyland concern.

However, it was considered that there was a case for the development of a lighter and simpler type of vehicle described as a railbus and examples were ordered from

five makers, one of which was Bristol Commercial Vehicles Ltd. They had built two two-axle underframes numbered RBX1 and 2, each with a single Gardner 6HLW engine, and for which ECW built the bodywork, given numbers EX1 and EX2 in a series henceforth to be used for experimental projects. The bodies were built separately and mounted on jacks to allow the underframes, delivered from Bristol by road, to be manoeuvred beneath them. Although relatively light and small by rail standards, they were larger than anything ECW had previously built, measuring 42ft. 4in. long and 9ft. 3in. wide with a weight

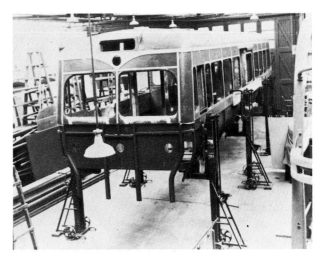

One of the two railbuses for British Railways under construction. The tall jacks were used to allow the underframe delivered from Bristol to be rolled underneath.

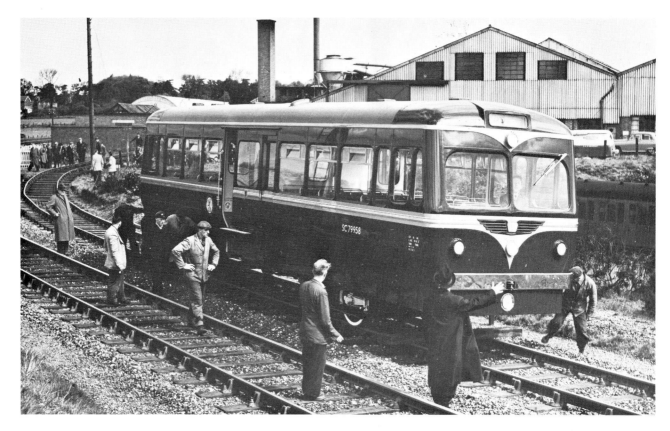

The first of the two Bristol-ECW railbuses is driven out of the ECW factory after completion and painting in the dark green livery then used for British Railways stock of this general type in 1958. The body was given the number EX1 in a new series henceforth used for experimental work. The driver is B. J. (John) Cox, then of Bristol Commercial Vehicles and responsible for the project 'from the first nut and bolt', as he described it recently, but in later years becoming well-known as the representative of Leyland Bus on various national and international engineering committees.

of 13.5 tons complete. There were 56 seats for passengers and driving positions occupying the 'left' corner (as viewed from within) at each end, passenger entry being by sliding doors centrally placed on each side, with a vestibule area for parcels or luggage.

The finished vehicles, numbered SC79958 and SC79959, were manoeuvred on to the railway track alongside the factory and, after testing, delivered for service in BR's Scottish Region on 12th August and 17th November 1958 respectively. They operated mainly between Aviemore and Elgin but continued in service only until October 1966, British Railways having decided not to pursue the railbus idea further at that stage. The two

vehicles were then scrapped, an undignified end to a unique venture for both Bristol and ECW.

A few months after the railbuses, ECW fulfilled a somewhat surprising contract to build a mobile laboratory body for use by British Railways' research department engineering division, based at Derby. A Bedford RLH four-wheel-drive chassis was selected to allow access to off-road sites alongside railway lines. Body number 10086 in the normal series was allocated and the vehicle delivered in March 1959.

The SU single-deckers

By contrast, another 'light vehicle' venture in which Bristol and ECW were involved a year after the railbuses were truly at the diminutive end of the scale. This was the SU (small underfloor) which as its designation implies was a venture using the mid-underfloor engine layout for a small-capacity bus. Its inspiration had been the introduction by the Albion concern, by then a subsidiary of Leyland, of its Nimbus model based on this concept,

The mobile laboratory body built on a four-wheel-drive military-style Bedford RLH chassis for British Railways was an unusual product for ECW, possibly a spin-off from the contact over the railbuses. It was numbered 1035S and registered 215 HRO in Hertfordshire, as was the practice for Midland Region vehicles, following a tradition going back to the establishment of its Road Motor Department at Watford by the London & North Western Railway.

The Bristol SU had much in common with the Albion Nimbus, but the Bristol engineers set ECW some problems by opting for a high-mounted front radiator. The rectangular grille may have been logical but its position gave an odd look to the completed vehicle, and imposed a shallow windscreen. Even so, the idea of a compact vehicle had merit for many of the more rural routes in Devon and Cornwall, traversing narrow and winding lanes as they do, and accounting for the repeat orders placed by the Western and Southern National companies. The initial entry of the type was in the 1959 programme, which called for sixteen of the SUS4A, with 30-seat bodywork (11384-99 built in batch 253), seven being delivered to Southern National and nine to Western National in January/February 1960. This one, 606 (678 COD) with body 11397, is seen leaving Penzance station on a special service to the airport at Land's End in July of that year.

The SUL4A, longer but, at 28ft. 2in., only a little more so than the immediate post-war L-type, appeared in the 1960 programme, with 29 examples of the 36-seat bus body (12020-48, in batch 277). Again, Southern and Western National were the customers, with eight for the former, including 617 (319 EDV) with body 12021, seen here ready for delivery from ECW in the latter part of 1960. The SU body was somewhat unusual among small buses in having a luggage boot at the rear, and the arrangement of a longitudinal seat over the front wheel arch left space for parcels, both features of value in a rural area with significant holiday traffic.

introduced in November 1955. The engine was, in effect, a four-cylinder derivative of the Leyland unit in the Tiger Cub model and the only engine of suitable size available in horizontal form.

The Tilling companies foresaw a need for a vehicle in this class and the SU used the Albion EN250 engine and other mechnical units as employed in the Nimbus. There were two lengths, the SUS model measuring 24ft. 4in., giving 30-seat capacity in bus form, while the SUL was approximately 28ft. long, the 36-seat bus version being

2in. over this length while the 33-seat coach was 2in. under. The overall width was 7ft. 6in. for both models. The main operators of the type were the Western National and closely-related Southern National companies run from the same headquarters in Exeter, who operated many rural services in the West Country and which had not operated the SC type. Between them they took a total of 133, comprising 89 SUL saloons, 28 of that model in coach form and sixteen of the SUS. In fact only 25 of the SUS version were built, the other nine going to Bristol Omnibus, but the SUL saloon was supplied to West Yorkshire (18 examples), Southern Vectis (8), United Counties (6), and United (5), with two

The first examples of the 33-seat coach version of the SU also appeared in 1960, eight with bodies 12059-66, built in batch 270, being split equally between Southern and Western National and delivered in September of that year. Though also designated SUL4A, they were a little shorter and had a different structure, the floor level being higher to allow all forward-facing seating. In consequence, the frontal appearance was better balanced, with grille set lower, no step in the profile and a slightly deeper windscreen. The entry door was of the inward-swinging coach type, and indeed the overall effect was not unlike a scaled-down MW coach. Southern National 406 (316 EDV), with body 12061, is seen at Ilfracombe in August 1962.

105

The 1961 version of the SU coach had more extensive use of brightwork than that of the previous year, the horizontal green stripe perhaps helping to give an illusion of greater length. At the front, a reshaped grille with polished strip enclosing the headlamps was 'different' but whether an improvement is perhaps a matter of opinion. Nine vehicles were built with bodies 12766-74 in batch 294, four for Southern National and five for Western National, all delivered in May-June 1961, the former's 410 (924 GUO) with body 12768 being seen in Plymouth bus station. Originally the destination box was like that of the previous type shown overleaf, but had been modified to include a route number box as seen here.

of the coach version going to United Welsh. Production continued from early 1960 to 1966, though annual output was modest, the initial year's delivery of 36 being the maximum, with a drop to eleven in 1964 before climbing to 28 in the last year. The first SUS saloons were delivered on 22nd January 1960, three going to Southern National and one to Western National, two coaches being delivered on 9th September 1960, followed by three saloons on 23rd of that month.

Lodekka developments

The LD-series Lodekka as put into production early in 1954 had proved highly successful, examples being supplied to all Tilling Group operators except Brighton Hove & District, and all Scottish Bus Group companies except Highland Omnibuses. There had been minor variations, as conveyed in illustrations, notably the version unofficially distinguished as Mark II with revised cab and front bulkhead window outlines introduced in 1956 and seven variations of platform design largely related to the absence or provision of platform doors, as well as vehicles with experimental features.

However, more fundamental changes led to the development of a second-generation series of Lodekka models. The first factor was an increase in the maximum permitted overall length for two-axle double-deckers from 27ft. to 30ft. which came into effect on 1st July 1956. By no means all operators considered they needed to take advantage of this increase at the time and the pressure for new vehicles to do so was not as urgent as with the corresponding increase in length of single-deckers in 1950. Even so work on a 30ft. version was put in hand and it is also worth recording in this context that an agreement between Bristol Commercial Vehicles Ltd and Dennis Bros Ltd concluded in 1956 allowed the latter to build chassis to the Lodekka design. A 30ft. chassis made up from Lodekka parts was displayed on the Dennis stand at the Commercial Motor Show of that year, a version incorporating some units of Dennis design going into production in the latter part of 1957.

Even so, the first 30ft. buses of Lodekka pattern were six Bristol chassis with Gardner 6LW engines which, complete with ECW bodywork, were delivered in October-

The 1957 ECW production programme, totalling 814 bodies, was the largest since 1948, and the Lodekka in its standard Mark 2 form outnumbered all other types put together at 417 units. The body numbers were quite fragmented, spreading from 9199 to 10011 but this range included batches of other types including the last K-types and the prototype 30ft Lodekka models as well as various single-deckers. They were built in batches 189, 200, 213-224, 231 and 232, with the usual spill-over from the preceding and into the following programmes. The Scottish companies took 121 examples, including the vehicle shown, delivered in the summer of 1957 to Alexander as RD37 (JWG 92), with body 9246. However, by the time it was photographed that company had been split into three, this vehicle joining the Alexander (Fife) fleet as FRD37 and taking that concern's bright red and cream livery.

The first 30ft-long version of the Lodekka was this example for Western National, delivered in October 1957. ECW records describe it as of type LLD, though called LDL in contemporary accounts based on Bristol information. The wheelbase was increased to 18ft 6in and the spacing of the body pillars revised to suit, but the rear overhang was noticeably longer than on later 30ft versions. It was 1935 (VDV 752) with chassis 134.102 and body 9577. The offside view shows the absence of an opening window in the first bay of the lower deck, this being due to it being a top-hinged emergency exit, required by regulations on a vehicle of this length in addition to that in the nearside of the rear-end, which, incidentally conformed to Lodekka platform design No. 3.

November 1957. The wheelbase was increased from the standard LD figure of 16ft. 8½in. to 18ft. 6in. There is some confusion about the correct designation of these vehicles but ECW records show them as LLD, though some sources, evidently of Bristol origin, quote LDL. As they differed from a subsequent design using that designation, it is proposed to follow ECW practice in this volume. The body was extended by using longer bays for the four main windows (thus allowing the pillars fore and aft of the rear axle to extend down to the chassis outriggers as before) and using a half-length fifth bay, glazed on both sides of the lower deck and extending into the upper deck, which thus had two relatively short windows at the rear of each side. The seating capacity was increased to 70, the unladen weight of the first vehicle (body 9577), for Western National, which had the optional platform doors,

was 8 tons 7cwt. 1qr. It was delivered, initially to Bristol, on 16th October 1957, followed by one each for Hants & Dorset (9405), Thames Valley (9520), Notts & Derby (9439), Bristol Omnibus (9260) and a second bus for Western National (9578).

The foregoing six LLD-type vehicles formed part of the 1957 programme, which comprised some 417 of the standard 27ft. LD-type buses, the largest annual total of the type, a quantity which included Scottish orders for some 121 examples. In the event, however, this line of offering an extended version of the standard LD was not taken further, even though the basic model was to remain in volume production for two more years and on a reduced scale until 1962.

It was revealed by early 1958 that a new version of the Lodekka with virtually flat lower-saloon floor as well as

Another of the six 30ft Lodekka 'LLD' buses derived from the LD type was Notts & Derby 463 (13 DRB) with body 9439, delivered in November 1957, and seen in Nottingham the following August. Surprisingly, these vehicles were built alongside standard 27ft. examples in batch 217, which comprised 35 buses, as did all of batches 213-224. This one did not have platform doors, the platform design being No. 6.

having air suspension for the rear axle and air-pressure brakes, in place of the previous vacuum type, was under development. In addition a new Bristol engine, the BVW, was announced, this being of 8.9-litre capacity and revised in quite a number of respects as compared to the previous 8.1-litre AVW. Clearly this had potential for larger versions of the Lodekka, though there was also mention of a BHW horizontal version. In the event, only one of the latter was fitted to an MW, the prototype vehicle with 'shell' body mentioned earlier in this chapter – it was removed and replaced by a Gardner 6HLW before the vehicle was fitted out for normal service and supplied to Red & White in 1962.

The next step was the construction of a pair of prototype vehicles with chassis numbers LDX.003 and LDX.004 in the series which had begun with the original Lodekka prototypes – the 30ft. LLD buses built in 1957 had normal chassis numbers in the 134th sanction, being intermingled with standard 27ft. LD models. The chassis of LDX.003

was described as an LDS, being built to 27ft. length, and was fitted with ECW body EX3, completed for Crosville Motor Services and delivered on 23rd September 1958, becoming that firm's DLG949.

Perhaps the most immediately striking feature of its appearance was the absence of a conventional radiator grille, the front cowl of the chassis simply having a version of the winged motif associated with the LS and MW single-deckers. This was because of the Cave-Brown-Cave heating and ventilating system, there being two large intakes, one each side of the front destination panel feeding air to combined engine cooling and interior heating radiator units. The CBC system had been the subject of earlier installations on LD-type buses, but the elimination of the normal front grille was a new and controversial, if logical, feature. However, the vehicle was far more extensively redesigned than implied by this feature, even though the outline was much as before.

The new chassis had been extensively redesigned,

The first of the two Lodekka prototypes put in hand in 1958 was 27ft long and designated as an LDS model, of which eight more examples were built about a year later, though effectively it was also the precursor of the FS as put into production at the beginning of 1960. It had body EX3, and was based on chassis LDX.003, becoming Crosville DLG949 (285 HFM). Although it retained the general outline of the 27ft LD-type, it was quite different constructionally, not only having the flat lower-saloon floor which was a major aim, but also a new method of chassis construction at the rear which made it no longer necessary to tie in the body pillars near the rear axle with frame outriggers. This in turn meant that the pillar spacing could be revised, and on the 27ft version, the true four-bay body layout, much as in the experimental bodies built on K-type chassis in 1949 (see page 49) was revived. The hopper type of opening window, with tilting rather than sliding action, was becoming increasingly popular, being used on both this pair of prototypes.

Visually, the most dramatic change in the appearance of the LDS prototype was at the front, where the normal radiator grille was eliminated, its place being taken by the much less prominent winged emblem as used on contemporary single-deckers. This was logical, as the vehicle had the Cave-Browne-Cave heating system, which meant that there was no radiator in front of the engine, and hence no need for the grille. In effect, the radiator had been split in two and moved to occupy the space alongside the destination display, the set-up being similar to that on the earlier experimental installations, with outlets in the front sections of the upper-deck side panels. The result of the change in terms of appearance was controversial, to say the least, reminding some observers of certain early 'thirties trolleybuses such as the London United 'Diddlers', and seeming to exaggerate the size of the bonnet assembly. This photograph was taken when it was returned to Bristol before delivery to Crosville, the destination blind suggesting that it was operated on a Bristol Omnibus Co route to Bridgwater, though the BOC blind did not fit properly in the box as that company did not conform to the Tilling standard in this respect.

with main sidemembers even lower than on the LD version, and at the rear the close co-operation with ECW had enabled an ingenious design to be evolved which combined the framework for the rear air suspension with inner and outer wheel arch members to be built into the body. As a result the pillar spacing was not directly governed by the rear axle position, and the LDS had four longer bays than the LD, eliminating the short one just ahead of the rear platform.

The second of these prototypes, on chassis LDX.004 and with body EX4, was designated LDL. This was quite

different to the six LLD vehicles of 1957, even though the body was outwardly very similar, again seating 70 passengers. The revised 'flat-floor' construction made it possible to accommodate a longer wheelbase, understood to have been 19ft. 0in., reducing the long rear overhang of the earlier LDL design. This vehicle had conventional ventilation and hence a normal radiator grille, also differing in not having platform doors. It was supplied to Eastern National, becoming fleet number 1941, on 3rd March 1959.

The 1958 double-deck production programme was

At first glance, the LDL prototype with body EX4 on chassis LDX.004 completed early in 1959 as Eastern National 1941 (236 LNO) looked similar to the previous six 30ft Lodekka buses, such as the Notts & Derby example shown on the opposite page, with similar spacing of the body pillars. However, the clue to its quite different design is seen in the position of the rear axle, set back and no longer sitting directly under the fourth main bay of the body. As with the equivalent 27ft design, the cradle for the rear axle, complete with its air suspension, was designed to be built into the body structure in a way which did not need the pillars to run down to meet chassis outriggers, and of course internally there was the benefit of the flat floor design, thus making this effectively the prototype for the later FL type. Both these two prototypes had Gardner engines, the full chassis designation in this case being LDL6G.

The standard Lodekka body continued to be the LD in its Mark 2 form through the 1958 programme. The numbers were down on the previous year's total, with 243 such bodies built, of which 74 went to Scottish companies. David Lawson Ltd continued to operate as a subsidiary of W. Alexander & Sons Ltd, and the first five of a batch of 20 numbered in the latter's fleet system were actually owned by Lawson and supplied in that concern's crimson and cream livery, though with typically Alexander cream wheels and gold lining, after completion in batch 224. They included the examples seen ready for delivery from Lowestoft in the summer of 1958, RD52 (KWG 605) with body 10150 being nearest the camera.

again almost all of LD-type Lodekkas of the Mark 2 body style, but did include eight further examples of the LDS type which were also the first Lodekka buses for the Brighton Hove & District fleet. In most respects they were similar to the Crosville LDS prototype, though three were of the convertible open-top type, a concept introduced by ECW in 1938, as illustrated on page 110 of my previous book on ECW and of which there had been earlier Lodekka examples these being eight LD6G for Crosville in 1956, followed by six LD6B for the same operator in 1959. The BH & D vehicles were body numbers 10179-81, the five with fixed-roof bodies being 10174-78, all eight being delivered in April-May 1959, among the last in the 1958 production programme. They all had CBC heating and, as built, lacked radiator grilles. However, overheating was experienced and conventional grilles were quite soon fitted, together with engine fans to give air circulation within the bonnet.

A further development was the introduction of versions with front-entrance layout – increasingly described as forward-entrance to distinguish such vehicles from those with entrance ahead of the front axle. Once again the Dennis connection played a part in the sequence of events as that concern had received a request for such a version of the Loline. Bristol had produced drawings for a Lodekka of this layout towards the end of 1957 but had not proceeded further as the Tilling group had not made a firm decision to adopt the type. So the drawings were passed to Dennis, which exhibited a forward-entrance Loline at the 1958 Show. However, this had a two-step entrance, which was regarded as a retrograde feature from the original Lodekka idea, and the design was developed to give a one-step forward entrance, by further modifying the frame design.

By this stage it had been agreed that the new generation of Lodekka models which had the flat floor would be given type designations in a new F series. Two further prototypes were produced, one in particular of which was to set the pattern for a major part of Lodekka output in the 'sixties. Oddly enough, despite their importance, they had 'normal' chassis and body

A minor change adopted at this stage but often applied retrospectively to earlier Lodekka models was the shortening of the front mudguards, it having been found that brakes could become unduly hot due to the lack of air flow. Midland General was among a minority of operators who continued to specify the 58-seat capacity, 475 (260 HNU) with body 10307, being one of three LD6G bodied in batch 234 and delivered in November 1958. Lodekka buses for Tilling companies in the 1958 programme were numbered in the series 10174-222 and 10224-351, the number 10223 being among the occasional blanks. The relationship of serial numbers to batch numbers was subject to the usual instances of carry-over between years but batches 231-237 included the main 1958 LD output, with some Scottish buses in 222-4 and some later deliveries, extending into mid-1959, in 254-6.

Brighton Hove & District's order for eight Lodekka buses was not only that operator's first, eliminating the only instance of a Tilling company not using the model, but effectively the first bulk order for the new generation of the model. They were LDS6B models with the new Bristol BVW engine, the vehicle shown, 6 (OPN 806) with body 10176, being one of the five of fixed-roof type and hence in Brighton red and cream. As delivered in the spring of 1959, all had CBC heating without radiator grilles, and hopper windows were fitted not only to the sides but also upstairs at the front. Note the London 'ear' type flashing direction indicator, mounted just above the first lower-deck side window.

It so happened that 1959 was a hot summer and operation in town traffic revealed a tendency to overheat on the 'no grille' LDS6B buses in Brighton. During 1960 and 1961, they were fitted with standard radiator grilles, which, with engine fans, improved the air flow through the bonnet and overcame the problem, as well as causing sighs of relief from those bus enthusiasts who found the original design unacceptable! In addition, at about the same time, the forward-facing hopper vents were replaced by the standard 'push-out' type of top-hinged vent, and the flashers were repositioned nearer the front corners of the body. Here one of the convertible open-top buses, 3 (OPN 803) with body 10181, shows all three modifications.

As sometimes happens, a vehicle which proved to have historic significance was treated as little more than routine, not being considered worthy of experimental number status. This was the first FLF-type Lodekka, chassis 156.001 of type FLF6B with body 10866, seen here, duly registered 995 EHW, ready for dispatch from ECW in October 1959 but not yet bearing the Bristol Omnibus Co fleet number LC8540, in the manner usual with buses for that fleet. The appearance was very much as was soon to become familiar as the FLF grew in popularity, with rather upright front and rear but a generally purposeful look – the radiator grille lesson had been learned.

111

Comparison of the three-quarter rear views of the FLF and FSF prototypes shows how the difference in length was achieved, the front-ends of the two types being similar. On the FLF for Bristol Omnibus, there were five full-length bays, that immediately behind the cab accommodating the staircase and entrance, with a short rearmost bay to make up the required length. The effect this had on the shape of the rearmost upper-deck side windows was perhaps not ideal but standardisation of components was beginning to influence ECW design considerably, and this window shape was to remain characteristic through the later VRT era. The FSF prototype, with body 11093 built for West Yorkshire as its DX82 (YWW 77) a little under three months later, had a tidier appearance, with four main bays plus one of almost full length at the rear. It was fitted with the Bristol engine and was thus an FSF6B.

The opening window arrangements of the two buses were noteworthy, the FLF prototype having hopper windows at the sides but the push-out type at the front of the upper deck, but the FSF had sliders at the sides and hopper at the upstairs front, and operators continued to have the option for either throughout the model's life. The FLF appears not to have had flashers as built, but the FSF had the 'orange segment' type then coming into widespread favour for buses.

numbers, the chassis in question being 156.001 and 156.002. The first, which received body number 10866, was the original FLF, the designation signifying Flat-floor, Long, Front-entrance, this being a 30ft. vehicle seating 70. It was for Bristol Omnibus and was delivered as fleet number LC8570 on 24th October 1959. The other vehicle was a 27ft. 'short' equivalent, seating 60, designated FSF and having body number 11093, delivered as West Yorkshire DX82 a little later, on 9th January 1960.

Even so, the two designs were closely related. The appearance and many detail features had obvious affinity to previous Lodekka practice, yet there was much that was new in addition to the move of the entrance itself. The front profile was more upright, this being necessary to accommodate a row of seats with adequate headroom in front of the staircase on the upper deck. The entrance, with a sliding door as originally built on both these vehicles, occupied one standard-length bay, and the FLF had four

further such bays plus a short one at the rear, producing the characteristic unusually short rearmost upper-deck side window which was to be found not only on production FLF buses but was to continue as a feature of many subsequent ECW double-deckers, most notably the VRT. The rear profile was also more upright than on rear-entrance Lodekka models. The side window arrangement of the FSF had three standard bays behind the entrance and then one of almost full length, giving a rather tidier effect. Within, the staircase design was such as to accommodate the protrusion of the gearbox beneath its lower steps.

Overall, the FLF in particular was to prove to suit the needs of many of the Tilling and Scottish companies. However, the sliding entrance door on the prototypes was not considered satisfactory. Both vehicles were soon afterwards fitted with double jack-knife doors during return visits to Lowestoft, being re-delivered in both cases in May 1960. Only five further FLF models, built for Thames Valley in 1960, and with coach seats, were constructed with sliding doors.

Meanwhile, the 27ft. rear-entrance flat-floor model, in effect what had been the LDS, now re-designated FS, went into production at the beginning of 1960, 40 such

The FLF and FSF prototypes, like other non-standard vehicles, spent some time in development work before entering regular service. The sliding entrance doors originally fitted were considered unsatisfactory and both buses returned to ECW for them to be replaced with the jack-knife doors which were to be standardised in production. The open intakes of the CBC heating system were replaced by slatted grilles similar to those at the sides. Both vehicles were redelivered in May 1960, the work done being covered by Rebuild numbers R750 and R757 respectively. The FSF, West Yorkshire DX82, is seen in service in Otley in May 1962. Oddly enough, West Yorkshire did not take to the front-entrance Lodekka, preferring the rear-entrance model and standardising on the FS6B for its subsequent needs. In 1967, an exchange was arranged with the United company under which it went to that fleet in exchange for an FS6B of similar age.

buses being produced as part of the 1959 programme. In most cases these were delivered as part of orders which had been placed for LD models and following on from deliveries of that type – only Brighton Hove & District received an all-FS delivery, twelve vehicles following on from the essentially similar LDS buses already in service. The first FS to be delivered was an FS6B, with body 10973, for Hants & Dorset – fleet number 1436, delivered on 26th February. The first production examples of the FLF and FSF, in both cases for Bristol Omnibus, were delivered on 2nd July and 17th September 1960.

The final F-series variant was the FL, 30ft. long with rear entrance and thus a direct successor to the Eastern National LDL vehicle of 1959. The first production vehicle was Red & White L160 with body 11762, delivered on 16th December 1960. In the event, this was to prove the least popular of the F-series models, only a total of 45 such variants being built in the period up to 1963, Red & White being the largest user. The FSF did rather better, with 218 in total, but this too faded out of the picture from 1963.

It took a little while for the FLF to become firmly established – in the 1960 programme, the FS was still the most numerous choice, but from 1961 the FLF was the main Lodekka type in production.

The Scottish companies, apt to be a little conservative in such matters, continued to favour the LD and the 85 examples bodied by ECW in the 1960 programme and the 77 in 1961 (Nos. 12093-169), the last new examples, were

The end of the road for the LD-type Lodekka came in the 1959 programme, so far as Tilling group operators were concerned, and effectively deliveries had almost finished by the end of that year. A total of 212 were built in that year's programme for Tilling companies, the design not being altered save that most if not all had the hopper type of vent in the front upper-deck windows. Southern Vectis 563 (SDL 268), one of a batch of five LD6G for that fleet built in batch 256 and delivered in May 1959, was typical. The choice of platform design continued, this being of No. 6 type. The body number pattern was complex because of the choice of types, but the main batch numbers in which vehicles for Tilling companies were built were 256-262 though a final pair for Crosville were 10923/4, built in batch 266 and delivered in March 1960.

The 1959 programme included 96 Lodekka LD6G buses, all 60-seat, for Scottish Bus group companies (bodies 10752-847, built within batches 236/7 and 254-6), delivered between December 1958 and May 1959. Western SMT B1485 (MCS 774) with body 10833 was one of 27 for that fleet, this view showing the pattern of opening windows, in this case all hopper-type, with two each side in the upper deck.

The SBG preference for the LD6G continued through the 1960 programme, when 85 were supplied (bodies 11423-507, built in batches 263/4 and 266 in December 1959-May 1960) and into 1961, when a final 77 (bodies 12093-169 in batches 289-90) were delivered between March and July. Scottish Omnibuses AA761 (USC 761) with body 11484 was one of 25 with platform doors supplied to this fleet in the 1960 allocation. SOL was still using the SMT diamond as a trading symbol, permission to do so for a specified period having formed part of the agreement when the BTC purchased the business even though SMT continued as a quite independent business in the motor trade.

The FL type, with 'flat' floor, rear entrance and 70 seats, went into production in the 1960 programme, no further prototype beyond the Eastern National LDL of 1959 being thought necessary as the design was effectively the same. It proved to have limited appeal, unlike 30ft. rear-entrance double-deckers of other makes which were being built in quite large numbers at the time. The number built under that programme was 25, all FL6G, the bodies (11014/5, 11757-79) all being built in batch 283 and delivered between December 1960 and January 1961. Red & White was the largest user, taking 20, but Lincolnshire took five, of which 2390 (OVL 485) with body 11757, seen here, was numerically the first. That batch also included two for Western SMT (bodies 12091/2), the only examples supplied to a Scottish fleet, but these were in the 1961 programme, even though delivered almost immediately afterwards in February 1961 and a good illustration of how the relationship between programmes and batching became complicated.

The FS Lodekka was the direct successor to the standard LD, with 27ft. length and rear entrance, initial deliveries generally continuing body, registration and fleet number batches that had begun with the older model. The first 40 were included in the 1959 programme, 35 built in batch 265 and five carried over to 278, all delivered between February and June 1960, the body numbers distributed in a broad range between 10715 and 11101. For the 1960 programme, the picture was much tidier, with 137 FS bodies numbered in one sequence (11570-706) and built in batches 278-282, delivered between May 1960 and July 1961. Among them was West Yorkshire DX105 (9763 WU) with body 11690, glinting in the sun as it awaits delivery in September 1960. It was one of a number for this fleet with CBC heating. The trade plate has a Bristol mark, HT, doubtless issued to BCV, but it is thought that it may have been used simply to deliver the bus to Harrogate. The cab side had at last been simplified, all F-type Lodekka models having the straight waist at this point.

Brighton Hove & District, though late in taking up the Lodekka, thereupon began building up a large fleet, including three of the four F-type variants. Its 1959 programme allocation of twelve buses was unique for that year in being all-FS, though doubtless it was considered undesirable to introduce the LD into a fleet which had none. In the 1960 programme, there were five more examples of the convertible open-top type (11570-74) delivered in May-July 1960, and these were notable for having the first examples of the special rear platform introduced by BH&D, with a low-level step adjacent to the bulkhead. This was introduced with the sizeable population of retired people in the Brighton area in mind, some of them having experienced difficulty in climbing to the normal platform level. This proved possible partly because of the air suspension of the rear axle which was a feature of the F-type Lodekka, but it is noteworthy that the same principle, translated to a front entrance layout, was taken up over 20 years later in London and elsewhere. Seen here in restored condition, with top cover removed, is 10 (RPN 10) with body 11571.

all LD6G buses for north of the border. There was one further LD-type body built, in 1966, when a 1955 Crosville vehicle, that company's DLG797, was rebodied (16054) after a fire. With that final body, the total of the type built was 2,180, the largest group of bodies of essentially the same design among the various Lodekka categories.

Various optional features or minor modifications were to be found on Lodekka models of the late 'fifties to early 'sixties. The Cave-Brown-Cave heating system was quite a widely favoured option in this period, a few early examples beginning life with the 'no-grille' front-end, though the version with the normal Bristol radiator

Production of the FLF-type Lodekka began in July 1960 with batch 286 as part of the 1960 programme. The Bristol Omnibus Co Ltd took eleven FLF6B with body numbers 10867-77 which followed on from that of the prototype, also for BOC, completed in October 1959. They were of similar specification and were delivered between July and September 1960, the first to go out apart from one vehicle for Thames Valley which was also included in that batch and delivered in July. The bus seen here in company with the West Yorkshire FS6B shown on the previous page was the last of the batch, numbered LC8561 by the operator and registered 581 HHY. Output of FLF models continued in succeeding batches 287/8 of bodies 11418-22 and 11707-56, plus a development shell (12009) later completed for use by Eastern Counties, making a total of 67 in the programme, completed by January 1961. It was a fairly modest start, but the FLF was to grow in importance in succeeding years.

For the first couple of years it seemed that the 27ft. forward-entrance FSF might rival the FLF and FS in popularity. The 1960 programme included 62, with body numbers 11508-69, all 60-seat and mostly on FSF6B chassis. The bodies were built in batches 284/5 which might have been expected to imply that they would be completed before the initial production FLF buses, but delivery did not begin until September 1960 and was completed in February 1961. The main recipients of these early examples were Bristol Omnibus and its subsidiaries, which took 32 (including 19 FLF6G), and United with 20, but Brighton Hove & District and Cumberland took five each. Seen here is a Cumberland example with body 11547, which began life as 406 (503 BRM) but had been renumbered 502 when photographed. The so-called T-type destination display was becoming a popular choice and, although retrograde in the amount of information which could be displayed, if properly set looked tidier than more elaborate systems not fully used.

The 1961 programme's FS total dropped to 79, though that figure must be considered in conjunction with the final 77 of the LD type of similar general layout and size sent to Scotland. Western SMT took three FS6G (bodies 12170-2) 'tacked on' to batch 281 and delivered in April of that year, though it was mainly the FLF6G that subsequently attracted Scottish Bus Group orders. Another unusual order was for four 'convertibles' (12286-9) in cream livery on FS6G chassis for Bristol Omnibus use on the Weston-super-Mare sea front service. The remainder (12333-7, 12366-70, 12392-451 and 12573/4) were for other Tilling companies, some of which were trying out batches of FS, FSF and FLF before settling on future needs. These were built in batches 282, 302 and 303 and delivered between April 1961 and February 1962. Among them were 19 for Eastern Counties, still wedded to the 5LW engine and hence of type FS5G, including LFS24 (1124 PW) with body 12399 seen here. There was some divergence in thought about destination display at this period within Tilling fleets, ECOC favouring the 'side-by-side' type shown.

The FL type was down to single figures in the 1961 programme, and if the pair of vehicles for Western SMT already mentioned as built immediately after the previous year's programme are set aside, it reduced to one order for six FL6B models for Hants & Dorset (12567-72) which comprised the entirety of batch 304 and were delivered in November-December. Seen here in NBC corporate livery in August 1976, but still looking very sound, is 1468 (4391 LJ) with body 12570. The opening windscreen of buses of that era was an asset to the driver in hot weather – the visor above it was a Hants & Dorset characteristic, added by that company. Note the illuminated advertisement panel, quite a common feature for a time until killed off by lack of demand.

Although the 1961 programme FSF total of 92 was the peak for this model, it was falling behind the FLF and the combined figure for FS and LD. There was another case of a Scottish order going out early and being added to a batch mainly of the previous year's allocations. In this case it was Central SMT which took seven FSF6G (12260-6) put into batch 285 and delivered in March-April – this was the only Scottish company to take examples of the FSF. The remainder, with various numbers between 12284 and 12608, were in batches 305-8, delivered between July 1961 and May 1962 – among the last was Midland General 509 (449 SNU) with body 12356, one of ten FSF6G and the only examples of the type for this company, though ten more went to the associated Mansfield District fleet. Note the alternate hopper and sliding vents, a not uncommon idea at this stage.

Eastern National broke new ground with three 55-seat coach versions of the FLF6B, using the rear of the lower deck for luggage racks. The coach seating reduced the upper-deck capacity by one from bus versions but only 18 were accommodated downstairs. Seen here at Victoria is 1610 (186 XNO) with body 12522. There were 155 FLF types in the 1961 programme, the remainder being buses for various Tilling fleets built in batches 288, 309-12 and 328/9.

The lack of either panel joints or mouldings was particularly evident at the rear, giving an effect almost like that of a toy. Doubtless because of the ease of moulding, it was decided to revert to the slight turn-under of the rear skirt, akin to the original SC prototype.

After a period in service, it was decided to paint Eastern Counties' glass-fibre SC, using almost the standard style of livery for the model, though the windscreen surround remained red. The different pillars continued to be evident as an identifying feature.

outline soon became standard. Rear-entrance models continued to be divided between those fitted with doors and with open platforms. Experiments on small numbers of vehicles with cream rather than black rubber for window glazing in 1960/61 led to standardisation on cream from 1962. Also in 1962, the radiator grille was changed from the version with flat surrounds to a slightly more elaborate moulded shape. The story of subsequent Lodekka developments is continued in the next chapter.

Glass-fibre bodywork

Although the SC type was nearing the end of its production run, it was used for two noteworthy experimental bodies, outwardly almost indistinguishable from the standard stage carriage version, but with complete body shell constructed in glass-fibre reinforced plastics, often abbreviated to g.r.p. or simply glass fibre. During the 'fifties, it had been adopted very widely for the smaller sections of bodywork where the shape is complex and front and rear panels in particular, where its ease of repair was a merit in addition to the facility of moulding. However, construction of a complete bus body was a much more ambitious venture and although the floor

structure was conventional, the visible parts of the body were produced in large sections. The standard SC outline was maintained but most of the normal panel joints were eliminated, giving a very clean appearance. In addition, the colour was impregnated into the resin, offering the prospect of eliminating the need for painting.

The first body was numbered in the experimental series (EX5) and delivered to Eastern Counties as fleet number LC565 on 17th March 1960, being operated from Lowestoft depot so that ECW staff could monitor its durability. Its all-red livery made it immediately identifiable, but the window pillars were slightly thicker and the glazing more deeply inset than the standard version; the rear panel curved inwards towards the lower edge in a similar manner to the three SC prototypes rather than the production version.

The second vehicle was similar but all-green, being supplied to Crosville on 15th September the same year – it had a normal body number (11981) being the first of a batch of sixteen buses of which the rest were standard. Both vehicles were later repainted with the normal cream window surrounds, the Eastern Counties bus surviving in service until 1972, among the last of its age in the fleet, but the venture was not repeated.

The standard Bristol SC4LK with body constructed in aluminium had continued in production, with very few changes over the years. The 1959 programme included 46 buses (11338-83) built in batches 246 and 247, plus ten coaches (11328-37) in batch 245. In 1960, the last year of relatively large-scale production following the arrival on the scene of the SU type, there were 37 standard SC saloons (11982-12008, 12010-9) in batch 276 plus ten more coaches (12049-58) in batch 269. Crosville SSG665 (238 SFM) with body 11982 is seen awaiting delivery in October 1960. By the time delivery of its orders had been completed in March 1961, Crosville had a total of 79 SC models in bus or coach forms in service. Lincolnshire had a further seven buses (12736-42) which formed batch 300 in the 1961 programme, delivered in July-August.

Production of the Bristol MW continued with little fuss or publicity – few people in the industry outside the State-owned sector even knew the model name. The 1958 programme included 143 examples of the stage and express carriage versions (10056-9, 10104-6 and 10352-487), built in batches 238-242 and delivered between November 1958 and July 1959. Among them were three MW5G for Durham District Services Ltd, a company formed after three independent operators sold out to the BTC in 1950. The 'obvious' course of action would have been for their businesses to be taken over by United as the major Tilling group operator in the area, but this would have infringed an area agreement with Northern General Transport Ltd, the main local BET operator, so DDS was formed and run as a United subsidiary, using Tilling green livery, in contrast to the parent company's red. This one, with body 10105, had been DBU15 when new but had become DU15 when photographed.

The MW bus body design was modified with effect from the 1958 programme, the rear profile becoming similar to that used for the LS, with a slight curve from the waist level upwards, the rear windows also being revised in shape, with what was generally agreed to be considerable improvement. Seen here at Victoria acting as a relief on coach duty is Eastern National 476 (213 MHK), an MW5G with body 10399, dating from early 1959. It was one of a batch with 41-seat capacity equipped for one-person operation.

The Bristol MW was to continue as the principal basis for single-deck bodywork built by ECW from the late 'fifties into the early 'sixties, and indeed it was not until after the 1966 programme that the main output of bus bodies passed to the RE. The yearly totals of MW bus bodywork rose slowly but steadily from the 1957 programme figure of 111. By 1959 it was 127, with body numbers 11104-36/44-62/8-242, built in batches 242 and 249-252, and delivered from July of that year to the following March. United was a major user, taking 45 MW5G in that programme, among which was BU570 (570 LHN) with body 11228, seen about to leave the Feethams bus station in Darlington for Catterick with a good load of passengers in June 1960 when about six months old. The same BU classification was used for LS and MW buses, but after the fleet numbers for the former reached BU283, a new start was made at BU501 for the MW. The hopper type of opening window seen here was becoming more popular.

The express version of the MW body also continued, and after 44 in the 1959 programme, there were 20 in the 1960 one, of which Eastern National 525 (2736 VX), an MW5G with 41-seat body 11841 delivered in January 1961, and seen here in Colchester in July 1968, was typical, though the deeper-than-standard hopper windows were noteworthy. As usual, most of them were numbered among the total of 132 bus versions that year, so that 11780-919 were all bodies of the basically common outline, with 11964/5 and 11971-80 as higher-numbered express versions, the whole built in batches 271-5 and running from mid-1960 to March 1961 in terms of deliveries.

This view of another United MW, BU655 (5055 HN), with body 12667 dating from the summer of 1962, gives an opportunity to compare the effects on the frontal appearance when CBC heating was specified, the normal radiator, and the grille that went with it, being replaced by the higher-mounted, broader but shallower divided opening shown. The destination display had also been reduced, as was common at the time, the front dome becoming similar to that usual on the express version. Overall, some of the balance of the original had been lost. Another significant feature was the 'pay as you enter' sign – what was then called one-man operation was becoming very common on buses of this size. It was one of 30 more MW5G for United out of the 1961 programme of 126 buses and 34 express bodies on MW chassis (12575-607/9-735) built in batches 295-9. This time production took longer, spreading from July 1961 to September 1962.

Profound shock is the only way to describe the general reaction to the new ECW coach design for the Bristol MW, introduced in prototype form on three coaches on MW6G chassis for the Tilling fleet delivered in September 1961. Gone was the smooth outline and instead there was a very 'fussy' front-end, with oval grille, for which the inspiration appeared to be that introduced by ERF on its lorry cab of 1956. The windscreen glass was curved but quite shallow and the profile, basically quite upright, had quite a pronounced step below the screen and a slight peak effect above. One description, not flattering in the context of the times, was 'tramlike', yet from it a remarkably effective style was to evolve. This was the second one, 4 BXB, with body 12222, the third, 12223 on 5 BXB, being similar with 34-seat capacity.

Chapter six: The Innovative 'sixties

Development of the RE

The early 'sixties were a time of major change in bus design, with particular emphasis on single-deckers so far as ECW was concerned, even though the Lodekka remained the most numerous type in production. There were two main reasons for this, one being the increase in the maximum permitted overall length to 36ft., which came into effect on 1st July 1961. Secondly and at the same time the width limit was slightly increased from 8ft. to 8ft. 2½in., these changes being intended to standardise with widely-accepted European limits of 11 metres by 2.5 metres In theory, this length increase was equally applicable to double- as well as single-deck vehicles, but weight limits kept the former category to more modest increases, if any, for the time being. At first, ECW did not increase the dimensions of existing models. In addition, what was then usually called one-man operation was legally permissible only on single-deckers at that time.

The idea of replacing double-deckers with large-capacity single-deckers had attracted attention when the 30ft. length for the latter had come into effect in 1950. To some degree, it had happened as numbers of passengers had fallen, but a 45-seat vehicle was not a match for even a 55-seat double-decker, and generally speaking the idea of relying on an increased proportion of standing passengers had not proved acceptable. The 36ft. single-decker increased the possibilities, especially if the driver could deal with fare collection, thus eliminating the need for a conductor. This was to be the subject of lengthy negotiations with the trade unions, but even the potential savings caused many operators and manufacturers to take a greater interest in developing single-deck designs for a

time, not least the Tilling companies and Bristol/ECW.

Some manufacturers simply produced lengthened versions of existing mid-engined models, with suitably uprated components, but Bristol and ECW took a bolder line. A completely new model, the RE, with rear underfloor engine, was developed and an announcement made in July 1962, by which date the first chassis was at ECW. The RE was to prove very successful, unlike some other early ventures in rear-engined layout, and although the Tilling group did not gain the benefit of the 36ft. length until a year or two later than other operators which used mid-engined models, the long-term benefits were considerable.

Thus ECW's output showed little change at first, with the Bristol MW continuing as the main single-decker alongside the F-type Lodekka models as the double-decker content, and the lighter SU and the last few SC making up the overall picture. In general, these were to designs established in the late 'fifties, apart from minor details such as the use of cream glazing rubber as standard from 1962.

A hint of what was to follow, however, came in a new coach design for the MW, introduced in prototype form in 1961, soon after the final deliveries of the familiar style which, with minor changes, had continued since the LS period. The new design had a controversial appearance, abandoning the flowing curves in profile of the previous design for a more upright style, with windscreen glass curved laterally but almost upright in profile and slightly recessed in the body contour, with a curved step beneath it. At the rear, the effect was almost reminiscent of the 1951 RFW coaches built for London Transport, with

At the rear, the 1951 prototype body on MW chassis had a distinct echo of the 1951 'Continental' design – compare with page 73 – both having a three-section rear window using curved glass for the corner sections. The stepped waist was a surprising feature, reminiscent of the 'thirties, and evidently it was not felt to be sufficiently marked on this first vehicle, body 12221 on Tilling 1 BXB, for the depth of the upper stripe was slightly increased on the remaining two, which also had 34-seat rather than 39-seat capacity. The prominent waistband, emphasised by polished mouldings, was to be developed as a key feature in the subsequent RE version.

curved glass corner windows flanking a rectangular centre window, the cantrail moulding continuing unbroken right round the rear of the vehicle. There was a slight step up in the waistline at the fourth main bay, an unusual feature on a coach at that time, and another new feature was the oval radiator grille.

Overall, the effect was widely agreed to be not the happiest of ECW designs, yet some of the ideas it incorporated were to be developed in a much more successful way. Three examples (12221-3) were built, all on MW6G chassis, for the Tilling Transport fleet and following on numerically from a pair to the previous

design. The new-style vehicles comprised one 39-seater and two seating 34, all delivered in September 1961.

The design was put into production in the 1962 programme, the 82 examples being delivered to twelve of the Tilling companies during that year. There were slight changes to the original design, most notably the incorporation of a grille outline which was a smaller-scale approximation to that being used on the Lodekka up to that time (though not the latest version then on the point of being introduced). Some minor variations to suit operators' requirements were to be found in such respects as destination display or door design, and the vehicles for

The contrast with the standard coach design familiar for seven years was immense. The 1961 output included the final 78 (12173-217/9/20/4-54) of the latter, built in batches 291-3 delivered during March-July 1961, with the usual minor variations but much as previously produced. Representative was United Counties 201 (YBD 201) with body 12230, one of four with 34-seat capacity for this fleet, seen before delivery – alongside is one of the rare FL-type Lodekka 30ft. rear-entrance buses, Red & White L660, this company being the largest user of the type.

The new MW coach design was put into production in the 1962 programme with minor modifications, the most obvious of which was the adoption of a grille outline a little nearer to a recognisable Bristol shape. The vent in the front dome was moved under the peak. There were 82 bodies (12788-839/45-74) built in batches 313-5 and supplied to twelve of the Tilling fleets in February-June 1962. The vehicle shown, 10 DLY, had begun life as one of five for Tilling but was one of three transferred to Eastern National in May 1965, this one becoming 356, the others following in 1968 – the Tilling coach fleet was closely linked to Eastern National in this period.

Royal Blue and United were in the operators' characteristic liveries.

The 1963 programme batch of MW coaches were generally similar but took advantage of the revised length regulations (which also increased the permitted overhang) to a minor degree by being 31ft. long, this being added at the rear, the rearmost half-bay becoming three-quarter length, more noticeable on the offside where the emergency door was now much wider. Delivery of these 134 coaches began as early as November 1962 and was completed by May 1963.

Meanwhile, the two prototype RE chassis had arrived and been bodied. REX.001 was a bus version, with chassis of RELL type (Rear Engine Long Low-frame) with Gardner 6HLX engine, this being a horizontal version of the 10.45-litre 6LX type by then available, and with other features such as synchromesh gearbox and air suspension. The chassis, completed by the end of April 1962, was delivered to ECW on 4th May. The body built for it (EX6) departed from previous ECW practice in several respects. The idea of an almost upright windscreen, curved quite markedly in a lateral sense, was similar to the new MW coach

The new-generation single-decker arrived in the form of the first Bristol RE prototype, chassis REX.001 with 54-seat bus body EX6, seen here in its official portrait; it was delivered, initially to Bristol Commercial Vehicles, in September 1962. The upright front-end with laterally curved windscreen had a little of the same line of thought as the MW coach of two years earlier, but in a much cleaner and more functional form, with smooth outlines. The extra length by then permitted helped in creating a visually attractive design. It was to operate as United BR1 (7431 HN).

The rear view of the prototype RE bus caused some surprise, for ECW had favoured placing the emergency exit of single-deckers at the side, at either front or rear, for standard designs since 1946. Here, however, the centre-rear position seemed logical, since the engine was positioned 3ft forward of the extreme rear. This was possible because of the way the drive was taken forward to the gearbox, mounted ahead of the rear axle, and then back to the axle. The use of curved glass allowed the overall shape of the rear to have a gentle curvature above waist level. Alternate hopper and sliding vents were used for the opening side windows. Dimensions were 36ft by 8ft 2½in.

design, but it was considerably deeper and mounted flush to the body outline, giving a much cleaner appearance. The chassis, as was to remain usual on Bristol rear-engined models, had a front-mounted radiator, and a grille for this, itself of a new shape, was built into the front panel.

At the rear, the appearance was more traditional, though the use of an emergency exit door centrally placed in the rear bulkhead, with a window each side, was not one generally associated with ECW – the appearance was 'softened' by the glazing in the three rear-facing windows being of curved glass. There were six main bays, with a smaller seventh and short final shaped side window.

The floor level in the front half of the vehicle was relatively low, with longitudinal seats over the front wheel arches, the seating ramping up rearwards to a higher level, allowing forward-facing seating over the rear axle. A single entrance was provided at the front, the seating capacity being 54. It was completed for United, being given the fleet number BR1, though initially delivered to Bristol on 19th September 1962 and not going to United until 16th November.

By then, the second RE chassis, REX.002, this time of RELH type (Rear Engine Long High-frame) though with similar mechanical specification to the first, had arrived on 10th November. It was fitted with a 47-seat coach body, again numbered in the experimental series as EX7. In this case, the body was an extended version of the contemporary MW coach design, with slightly longer

The RE coach prototype, with chassis REX.002 and body EX7, showed an obvious affinity to the contemporary MW version, though gaining from the extra length and using the latest version of the Lodekka radiator grille, giving a much stronger character to the front end. The stepped waist was used, with five main side windows, both features not carried over into the production version. The vehicle was delivered to Bristol in March 1963 and to the operator the following month. By that date, South Midland was run as part of Thames Valley, which was legal owner of this vehicle, numbered 867 in the latter's fleet and registered 521 ABL. Even so, it passed to City of Oxford Motor Services Ltd when the latter took over responsibility for South Midland in 1971.

The new type of radiator grille had appeared on Lodekka deliveries to operators from August 1962, being combined with a revised arrangement for the registration plate, neatly combined with a step to allow access to the winding handles for the destination blinds. This example was one of the first, being delivered to Mansfield District Traction Co that month, and had the three-aperture destination display usual on Midland General group double-deckers. It was one of ten FLF double-deckers for that operator, five, of which this, 545 (241 MNN) with body 13168, was the first, were FLF6G and the rest FLF6B. The FLF had become the most popular Lodekka variant, with 287 produced in the 1962 programme (13046-118/25-262, 13494-518/49-99) built in batches 328-335 and delivered between March 1962 and April 1963.

window bays but retaining the stepped waistline. At the front, a bolder appearance was given by the use of the new-style radiator grille that had been standard on Lodekka chassis from the spring of 1962, mounted on a panel which accommodated the quadruple headlamps. Forced-air ventilation, a new system at the time, and based on airliner practice, was incorporated. Hence no opening windows were provided, except for the driver's signalling window, though three lifting roof vents were incorporated, a feature which was in growing favour at the time. This vehicle was supplied to Thames Valley for operation in South Midland livery, though again going initially to Bristol on 27th March 1963, spending almost a month there before delivery to the operator on 25th April.

In passing, it should be mentioned that from 1st January 1963, the road transport interests of the British Transport Commission were transferred to the newly-formed Transport Holding Company, BTC being dissolved. This change resulted from the Transport Act 1962, but in practice the day-to-day activities of the Tilling and Scottish Bus Groups, as well as British Road Services, did not alter appreciably. The same applied to

The FSF, on the other hand, was past its peak, with 52 in the 1962 programme (13024-45, 13519-48). Of these, 30 were for Central SMT, built early in the year in batches 307/8, the remainder comprising seventeen for United Welsh, including 364 (262 DCY), an FSF6B with body 13028, awaiting final details before delivery in October with the rest of the batch and five for Durham District. Only eleven more of the type were built (14322-32 in batch 347), delivered in August/September 1963 to Central SMT.

The 1962 programme included the first deliveries of the FLF6G to Scotland – 25 for Scottish Omnibuses, 25 for the Alexander companies and 26 for Western SMT. Over the years, the Scottish Bus Group, as it became known from 1963, was to build up a total of 376 of the type. Among the first, in March 1962, was Scottish Omnibuses AA871 (YWS 871) with body 13495, seen here, the slatted type of CBC intakes and the rather sparse provision of opening windows considered adequate for the northern climate being evident. The General Manager of SOL at the time was Roderick MacKenzie, later to become the Director responsible for engineering matters for SBG, where his high regard for the merits of the FLF – "Roddie's favourite bus" – were to become legendary in later years, influencing the decision to swap the group's VRT models for ex-NBC FLF types.

By contrast, the other 30ft Lodekka variant, the FL, was at the end of the road, the final dozen being built in batch 337 and delivered in December 1962, there being six FL6B for Eastern Counties (13119-24) and six more, this time FL6G, for Hants & Dorset (13263-68).

There was an upsurge of coach production in 1963, and although the new RE attracted much attention, 102 out of the 134 were further examples on MW6G chassis, very similar to the 1962 pattern, but taking advantage of the greater freedom given by the relaxation in the permitted overall length. It was possible to build bodywork on this chassis to a length of 31ft., the limit being set by the maximum permitted overhang, so the design was extended at the rear. They were numbered 13600-25/30-78/80-705/28, and built in batches 338-40, delivery beginning in November 1962 and being completed by May 1963. Seen here is Midland General 282 (1379 R) with body 13649, one of six for this fleet and four for Mansfield District which had the forced air ventilation system then beginning to come into favour and hence dispensed with opening side windows. The dual fleet names aided use on either company's duties.

those of Bristol and ECW, though the change in organisation and slightly more 'commercial' approach of the THC paved the way for an important change later in the decade.

Production of RE models began with an initial batch of 32 RELH coaches included in the 1963 programme but delivery to operators did not begin until 19th October of that year with the first of a batch of ten for Bristol Omnibus, the vehicle in question being No. 2115 in that fleet, with chassis number 212.001 and body 13708. The general outline of the body was as introduced on the prototype, but the overall appearance was significantly altered by the adoption of a $4\frac{1}{2}$-bay layout, the elimination of the stepped waistline and standardisation on a livery which helped to emphasise the length with a deep waistband, usually in red or green, contrasting with the basic cream. The relief colour was also used for the panel surrounding the radiator grille and including the four headlamps. The seating capacity was usually 47, with quite generous spacing, but some examples seated 45. A noteworthy feature was the use of an exhaust-heated boiler to supply saloon heating, the Gardner engine's

efficiency meaning that the more normal diversion of water from the engine cooling system had been found inadequate. Included in this batch was a third prototype chassis, REX.003, delivered back to Bristol Commercial Vehicles in October 1963 as a shell (13736) and used as a test vehicle until completed by ECW under Rebuild No. R882 and delivered to West Yorkshire in February 1967 as fleet number CRG1.

The express version of the RE was also based on the RELH chassis and, unlike previous models, used the coach body shell, the only difference of any consequence being the use of a folding entrance door instead of the hinged type. The seating was usually directly comparable and in fact ten vehicles built for United and used on the London-Newcastle services were modified from 45 to 43, offering exceptional comfort. More usual was 47-seat layout but three for Midland General were of 51-seat capacity, also differing in having opening portions to the windows in each main bay, and a rear indicator.

Although 40 production stage carriage versions on the RELL version of the RE chassis figured in the 1963

'Ugly duckling turned into swan' might be a little too sweeping a description, but the derivation from the 1961 coach style as first developed for the MW into the production version for the RE two years later was a remarkable transformation. Seen above is the first production RE, Bristol Omnibus 2115 (861 UAE), which had RELH6G chassis 212.001 and body 13708, delivered from ECW on 19th October 1963. The changes from the RE coach prototype, and in particular the adoption of longer side windows, in accordance with a trend then under way in British coach design generally, coupled to the elimination of the step in the waist, contributed greatly to the overall effect. The bold use of a waistband in contrasting colour was a feature of most RE coaches and the Bristol vehicles, which carried the Bristol Greyhound fleetname reviving the name of a former subsidiary, with an appropriate symbol, looked particularly striking. The rear view shows 2119 of the same batch. The 32 examples in the 1963 programme (13626-9/79, 13708-27/9-32/6/8/9), all built in batch 341, were completed by January 1964, though body 13736, built on chassis REX.003 was a shell used by BCV for development until completed for West Yorkshire in 1967.

The express version of the RE was also built on the RELH6G chassis and generally differed only in the use of folding entrance doors instead of the inward-swinging hinged type . In the 1953 programme, 27 were built (14145-71) in batch 342 and delivered in the first three months of 1964. Three delivered to Midland General were more truly of dual-purpose character, uniquely having seats for 51 passengers and opening side windows (alternately hopper and double-slider), as well as a rear destination box, as shown here by No.30 (1384 R) with body 14155.

The production bus version of the RE, on RELL6G chassis, although also included in the 1963 programme, did not begin to appear until September 1964, when the first of the 40 vehicles, with bodies 14174-8 and 14182-216 built in batch 346 appeared, the last being delivered in November. All were 54-seat vehicles with a single entrance door at the front. United was the largest recipient, with 30 to add to the prototype already in that fleet, Lincolnshire took four and Thames Valley and West Yorkshire three each. The last-mentioned's first example, SRG1 (BYG 756B) with body 14214, is seen awaiting delivery, with the chassis of another RE alongside – the front-mounted radiator and low frame height are clearly seen.

programme, it was not until 11th September 1964 that deliveries began, with two examples for United, fleet numbers BR2 and 3, and two for West Yorkshire, that concern's SRG1 and 2, continuing until later in the year. The main recipient was United, adding 30 to the prototype delivered the previous year. The body design was slightly modified from that vehicle, the windscreen depth being slightly reduced and a bolder design of radiator grille adopted. This was of Bristol outline, though the surround was finished in the main body colour. All were 54-seat front-entrance buses but seven vehicles, for Lincolnshire and Thames Valley, differed from the rest in having the T formation of destination display (with single-line destination fitted over the route number) requiring protruding 'humps' at both front and rear, thus spoiling the otherwise smooth lines.

The late delivery of these vehicles was a symptom of a wider problem, for demand had been outstripping capacity, with the result that most bodies were not being delivered until the year after that planned. It was agreed that ECW's production programmes would be rearranged

so that, as far as possible, bodies would be delivered during the programme year. To achieve this, 1964 orders for single- and double-deck stage-carriage bodies were merged into the 1965 orders.

In consequence, the total number of bodies in the 1964 programme was only 368, about half the typical total for that period, including no MW or RE stage saloons, and with the Lodekka total well down. For 1965, by contrast, there were no coaches, this partly relating to the fact that, for some time, coach deliveries had been made early in the year to ensure availability for the seasonal demand for such vehicles. They were consequently less inclined to be behind schedule, so with a combined 1964-65 programme, the 1964 coach allocation had been built in the correct year.

An illustration of how the combined programme for 1964 and 1965 worked out for one operator is given by Eastern Counties, whose 1964 programme comprised 31 Lodekka FS and 17 MW saloons, plus 12 MW coaches already built before the review of outstanding orders. None of the allocation of MW saloons were built in 1964

Despite all the interest the new RE was creating, extending far beyond the State-owned sector to which it was confined by the restrictions on Bristol and ECW sales, the major volume of single-deck sales for both concerns remained with the MW. In the 1962 programme, the total with bus bodywork reached the record figure of 185 (12783-7, 13280-4, 13303-451/3-78) built in batches 319-323 and delivered between October 1962 and November 1963. Seen here at the factory alongside one of the first production RE coaches is Southern National 2623 (754 MDV), an MW5G with body 13415 delivered in October 1963, one of six for Southern National. The glossy green paintwork, still being 'properly' finished with black edging to the cream waistband, and elegant gold lettering, set standards far above those usual today. There were also 29 MW with express bodies (13269-79, 13285-302) built in batch 316 a little earlier, all delivered in 1962.

The SU type was another model which remained in production with little attendant publicity. The 1962 programme was noteworthy in there being three examples of the short SUS4A type, for the Bristol Omnibus fleet, with 30-seat bodies 13479-81, delivered in October of that year — hitherto there had only been one delivery of this type, in the 1959 programme and split between Southern and Western National. This view of the first, 300 (861 RAE), conveys how this body style continued to convey the origins of its rear-end design as the SC — the design was virtually unaltered though it was at about this period that ECW introduced the cream glazing rubber, producing an effect that was to remain an ECW characteristic for many years. They were grouped with six of the longer SUL4A for West Yorkshire (13482-7), another user new to the SU model, in batch 318. Further SU buses followed in the 1963 and 1964 programmes, when Keighley-West Yorkshire, Southern Vectis and United took small numbers.

There were also some 21 SUL4A coaches (12875-95) that year, built in batch 317 and supplied to Western National (15), Southern National (4) and United Welsh (2), the last-mentioned yet another newcomer to the type. Seen here is Western National 417 (267 KTA) with body 12881, seen in June sunshine before delivery.

There were a number of variations of detail features for the RE coach and express designs. United Counties followed its usual policy in using the latter for its express services to London and the specification shown here by 253 (ABD 253B) with body 14161 was fairly typical of those for various fleets, using one of the contemporary bus-type destination displays in conjunction with the folding entrance door, though the choice of what amounted to bus-style green and cream livery was less usual. It was delivered in March 1964, having been one of four for this fleet built in batch 342 as part of the previous year's programme, and is seen here in Nottingham in the following August. By then, a further six were being delivered from the 1964 programme.

For the 1964 programme, the MW coach was given a fresh look by modifying the frontal appearance, the step beneath the windscreen being eliminated and the glass increased slightly in height. The peak effect above the screen remained but the shape of the front dome was flattened in line with car styling trends of the time. The remainder of the standard design was unaltered, as conveyed by the official view of Hants & Dorset 897 (AEL 5B) with body 14468 when ready for delivery in April 1964. Altogether, the programme included 36 bodies to this general design (14436-71), all being 39-seaters on MW6G chassis and delivered between March and June 1964. There were no coaches in the 1965 programme as a consequence of the 'catching up' process described in the text. The MW did reappear as the basis for coaches in the 1966 programme when further generally similar vehicles were built, but the model was nearing the end of its run – more details will appear in the next volume.

Though included with the other MW coaches of the 1964 programme, the fourteen built for Crosville, including CMG513 (4222 FM) with body 14439 seen below, were significantly different in frontal appearance, with a distinct resemblance to the RE coach, or perhaps more precisely the express version as shown on the previous page. The RE-style front panel with Lodekka-type grille was fitted in conjunction with bus-style destination display above the windscreen. In addition, forced-air ventilation allowed the side windows to be of the fixed type. The type of door was another optional feature, Crosville favouring the inward-swinging hinged type which could be regarded as standard, whereas the Hants & Dorset coach used the folding type, more an 'express' feature.

The 1964 RELH coach programme comprised 37 vehicles (14472-505, 15136-8) built in batch 362 and delivered between April and July 1964, the big jump in body numbers of the last three, for Crosville, reflecting an aspect of the 'catching up' exercise. The general design was unaltered though there continued to be minor variations in the shape of the front dome, to suit operators' ideas on destination display. The series included the first examples for Royal Blue services, of which Western National 2358 (ATA 102B) with body 14503 is seen soon before delivery – there were ten for that company and four for Southern National, all seating 45. There were also 24 of the express version (14506-29) in batch 363 and delivered between May and September 1964. These vehicles offered comfortable travel with their air suspension and spacious seating, the Gardner 6HLX engine giving very relaxed cruising at up to 60mph, barely audible towards the front of the coach and not intrusive even at the rear. Performance compared well with the standards of the time and, as it happened, few Tilling companies then had express routes giving access to motorways, so maximum speed was more than adequate. No further RELH models were bodied until early 1966.

and they were coupled with three ordered for 1965, a series of 20 consecutive body numbers being allocated. Of the 31 FS, 14 were planned for production in 1964 and this quantity of body numbers allocated, the balance of 17 were coupled with nine planned for 1965 and 26 numbers allocated accordingly. Similar 'catch-up' patterns applied to other operators, though it seemed that the Scottish companies were permitted to order more or less normal quantities, at the expense of ECW's other customers.

The 1964 coach programme included 37 more RELH coaches, basically unaltered from those built in the 1963 programme though continuing minor variations of specification, mainly to suit differing destination display needs (though two listed as coaches for Hants & Dorset were unusual in having folding doors) and noteworthy as including the first batch in Royal Blue livery. There were also 24 of the express type with folding doors.

Also in the 1964 programme was a revised version of the MW coach, with almost literally a 'face lift' for the front end. The step in profile below the windscreen was eliminated, and the screen glasses were slightly taller, their upper edge now lining up with the top of the side windows. The peak above the screen remained, though the dome above was shallower. There were 36 vehicles, and in most cases the remainder of the design was otherwise much as the 1963 version, but fourteen for Crosville had the lower front panel to RE style, complete with grille as used on the Lodekka, and a destination display of bus pattern being incorporated in the front dome.

Despite the high regard the Bristol RE was attracting, the emphasis in the early and mid-'sixties in terms of ECW production remained with the Lodekka and particularly the FLF variant, with the FS as runner-up. This was in line with a national trend in which 1964 was

The MW continued as the main workhorse single-decker for Tilling group companies, comfortably outnumbering the RELL until it went out of production in 1966. The 1963 programme included 80 with bus bodies (14067-144, 14172/3) in batches 344 and 345, built between November 1963 and a year later, illustrating how output was falling almost a year behind the nominal date in the case of this type. The problem was overcome by omitting MW bus bodies from the 1964 programme and jumping to 1965. Eastern Counties took delivery of sixteen MW5G, of which LM601 (601 ENG) with body 14100 was one of the first, delivered before the end of 1963 and receiving a registration number without suffix letter. The suffix system began with letter A that year, but only a few were issued before the more general use began with B in 1964, the next vehicle in this batch, LM602, being registered AAH 102B.

Production of the RELL bus proceeded, though not at a particularly high rate. The 1963 programme for this model not having been completed until November 1964, it was omitted from the 1964 programme but in fact construction barely ceased, for delivery of the 61 bodies in the 1965 programme (15220-80, built in batches 367 and 368) began in January of that year and continued until November. All were again 54-seat vehicles with single doorway and on the RELL6G chassis. Among them were four for Lincolnshire, adding to the four already in service and again having the T-shaped destination layout. This was taller than the more usual side-by-side layout and was accommodated by sweeping the front dome upwards in the rather odd-looking shape shown – a similar protrusion was used at the rear and the overall effect did nothing for what was otherwise a sleek outline. The vehicle shown, 1208 (BVL 47C) with body 15223, has been preserved. In later years, output of RE buses increased immensely as will be described in the next volume but up to the end of 1965 the total in service was 102, including the prototype, over half of which were in the United fleet.

a peak year for double-decker deliveries to operators in Britain generally. The 1964-65 programme revisions made assessment of the trend rather difficult, but average rates of delivery of FLF models was 248 per year over the 1962-65 period, the corresponding figure over the same period for the FS being 135, that for the MW in bus form being 100 and the RE in bus form (not put into production until 1963, admittedly) just over 25. The short forward-entrance FSF and long rear-entrance FL versions of the Lodekka had both proved comparatively short-lived, production ending in the 1963 and 1962 programmes respectively, though the FSF, with a total of 218 built since 1959 was briefly quite popular, the FL much less so at a total of 45.

In general, the Tilling and Scottish companies standardised on the 70-seat FLF or 60-seat FS during this period. In addition to the convertible open-top versions of

the FS built at intervals for Brighton Hove & District, three of the Tilling companies took coach versions of the FLF. Eastern National favoured a 55-seat design, beginning with three vehicles in 1961, the rear of the lower deck being used for luggage accommodation, the rearmost side windows and those each side of the emergency door on that deck being replaced by panelling. Three more were produced with slightly more elaborate external finish in the following year's programme, which also included five for Crosville, and the 1963 programme included two more for Eastern National and five for Thames Valley, though these seated 65, lacking the extensive luggage space. Crosville took five more to its pattern in the 1964 series, and in 1965 Eastern National added two, this time with 59 seats.

However, a more fundamental modification to the FLF was produced, beginning in 1965 with eighteen

The Lodekka FLF was the most numerous type of vehicle produced by ECW during most of the early 'sixties. The 1963 programme included 232 (bodies 13884-14066, 14273-321) built in batches 335 and 352-8, and although the 1964 total was down as a consequence of the 'catching-up' exercise, the actual production rate remained high. There were 123 FLF models in the 1964 programme (14333-75, 14553-632) built in batches 355-7, 376 and 377. The 75 bodies produced from batch 376 onwards had the nearside front bulkhead window angled to improve the driver's vision of boarding and alighting passengers. Cumberland was one of several Tilling companies that took batches of FS, FSF and FLF buses before settling on the FLF, the example shown here in Keswick being 525 (AAO 575B) with body 14571 built in batch 376, one of four similar buses in the 1964 programme, delivered in this case in October 1964. The previous programme included three FLF6L for this fleet, with Leyland O.600 engines, part of an exercise also involving Bristol Omnibus with a similar batch, and perhaps a pointer to subsequent developments involving Leyland, Bristol and ECW. Cumberland reverted to the FLF6G, however, standardising on the Gardner 6LX, which was rare at this period, though common later.

The possibilities of coach versions of the Lodekka had been realised by Crosville in 1954, in the days of the first production LD types, and the FLF was chosen as a basis for further batches supplied in 1962 and 1964. One of the five examples delivered in June-July 1964, having been built in batch 357, was DFB149 (AFM 112B), an FLF6B with body 14592. Coach seats were provided for 55 passengers and the overall effect in cream and black livery with wheel trims and the illuminated signs below the leading lower-saloon side windows was quite glamorous, as seen in this photograph taken at Llandudno in July 1966.

The FS, though generally outnumbered by the FLF in terms of ECW's production from 1961, was still quite strongly in demand, several operators considering its combination of 60 seats and the more manoeuvrable 27ft. length about right for their needs. It was also felt by one school of thought that, as conductors were still required on double-deckers, there was much to be said for the rear entrance on a vehicle of this capacity. There had been 128 FS in the 1962 programme (12896-13023, built in batches 3246 and 336) and 185 in the 1963 one (13733-5/40-883, 14235-72, some completing batches 326 and 336 and others in 348-351 and 359). The 1964 programme, distorted by the catching-up exercise, actually had more FS, at 125, than FLF. They were numbered 14376-435 and 14633-97, again filling in batches 350, 351 and 359 and in 'new' batches 370 and 371.

The West Yorkshire Road Car Co Ltd and its associated fleets were still regular customers for the FS6B, this example being for Keighley-West Yorkshire Services Ltd, a company set up in 1932 jointly with Keighley Corporation when the latter's trolleybuses were replaced by motor buses managed by WYRC. It was KDX165, built as part of the 1963 programme and originally intended to be registered 576 EWX, following on from the rest of the batch, but when body 13874 was completed in batch 351 it was April 1964 and a number under the new system had to be obtained. It was still incorrect, however, and the plate AWU 477B shown had to be changed to the correct AWU 467B. Visible behind are two FS6G completed under the 1964 programme for Central SMT, the vehicle directly behind being B184 (AGM 684B) with body 14393.

(15363-80) out of a batch of some 75 for Central SMT. This was an extended version, 31ft. 0⁷/₈in., long instead of the usual 30ft. in which seats for 78 passengers were provided. This had become possible due to the relaxations in length and overhang regulations. The FLF wheelbase of 19ft. 2¹/₄in. remained unaltered, the extra length being added to the rear overhang and in particular to the rearmost bay, which thus did not have the ultra-short proportions otherwise characteristic of the model.

The internal design was revised, the staircase ascending forward instead of towards the rear; the usual upper-deck capacity was increased by six to 44 and an extra pair of seats being added in the lower deck to bring its total to 34. Seat spacing was somewhat cramped and it is interesting to recall that 43 of the standard-length FLF models supplied to the same operator that year seated 68, the lower-deck total being reduced, this option being taken up in some other cases to allow more room for luggage. It should be mentioned in passing that engine options for the Lodekka at this stage included the Gardner 6LX, set to 135bhp for this application, as well as the 6LW. In 1963, three FLF models each for the Bristol and Cumberland fleets had been fitted with Leyland O.600 engines on an experimental basis, although subsequent events were to give this added significance.

Thames Valley retained standard red bus livery for its London-service double-deckers until early 1964 when five FLF6B for the London service (four in batch 355 and one in 358) were delivered in maroon and cream in the style used for the company's coach fleet at the time. These were not quite so elaborate as the Crosville or Eastern National versions, but had semi-coach seats for 65 passengers. The vehicle shown, D6 (ABL 118B) with body 14000, had another claim to fame, running with reflective front number plates with black-on-white lettering as an experiment in conjunction with the Road Research Laboratory several years prior to their general adoption.

Lodekka bodywork accounted for over two-thirds of ECW's output in the 1965 programme and over half were FLF types, of which 351 were built (14783-98, 14842-913/9-15081, 15281-380 in batches 375, 378-384), delivered in a period which virtually coincided with the calendar year, the peak output for the type. The most noteworthy from a design viewpoint were eighteen (15363-80) for Central SMT, built to take advantage of the maximum length possible on the FLF chassis and seating 78, as much as the rear-engined models of other makes of that period could accommodate, even if the seats were rather tightly spaced. The extra length could be described as beneficial from an appearance viewpoint, as the rearmost bay was extended, eliminating the rather pinched-looking final upper-deck window of the standard version. Seen here is BL274 (EGM 274C) with body 15364.

Appendix 1

Body number allocations – annual production programmes

1946	8810/8811 (Series 1), 1001-1578	580
1947	1579-2359	781
1948	2360-2728/2731-2747/2751-2788/2792-2864/2870-2901/ 2906-2917/2919-2969/2973-3386/3402-3441/3443-3447/ 3452-3454/3542-3546/3776-3778	1062
1949	2729/2730/2748-2750/2789-2791/2865-2869/2902-2905/ 2918/3387-3401/3442/3448-3451/3455-3541/3547-3775/ 3779-3850/3852-4061/4067-4194/4197-4254/4256-4270/4275-4280	843
1950	4062-4066/4195/4196/4255/4271-4274/4281-4685/ 4647-4961/4974-4989/5464	689
1951	4626-4646/4962-4973/4990-5463/5465-5693/5773-5781	745
1952	5694-5772/5782-6460/7191	759
1953	6461-7108/7114-7190/7192-7203	737
1954	7204-7624/7626-7698/7704-7808	599
1955	7625/7699-7703/7809-8250/8252-8432/8439-8443/8451-8462	646
1956	8463-8773/8776-8783/8804-8934/8938-9012/9023-9198	701
1957	8433/8784-8788/9013-9022/9199-9871/9874-9925/ 9943-10002/10004-10016	814
1958	9926-9942/10017-10063/10068-10080/10084-10146/ 10149-10168/10174-10222/10224-10492/10632-10642/ 10650-10663/10665-10667/10671-10676/10701-10704/ 10709-10714/10720-10751, EX1-4	558
1959	10715/10716/10752-10866/10878-11013/11016-11403/11407-11417	652
1960	10867-10877/11014/11015/11418-11966/11971-12077, EX5	670
1961	12078-12217/12219-12742/12748-12782	699
1962	12783-12840/12845-13451/13453-13599, EX6/7	814
1963	13600-13736/13738-14178/14182-14332	729
1964	14333-14697/15136-15138	368
1965	14698-14913/14919-15135/15139-15380	675
	Overall Total (1946-65)	14,121

*Actual year of build was quite often the following year to that quoted and occasionally was the previous year.

The 45-seat saloon bodies built on five Leyland Royal Tiger PSU1/13 chassis for United (7016-20) formed part of the 1953 production programme and were delivered in March-April of that year, earlier than usual within the programmed year for bus bodywork. The appearance was very similar to that of the Bristol-ECW LS model then in production, though in this case the body was built on a conventional chassis with the characteristic Leyland wheel nut guard rings and Royal Tiger badge as instant identification points. The last of the batch, LU5 (RHN 767) is seen at Marlborough Crescent, Newcastle-upon-Tyne, awaiting its turn to pull into the platform for the Carlisle service, for which the Royal Tigers were favoured, as vertical-engined Tigers had been before them, because of the hilly terrain at the northern end of the Pennines.

Appendix 2
ECW production 1946-65 by programme year and body type

Prog Year	Bristol K-Series & Similar Double-deck								Bristol L-Series & Similar Single-deck									ECW Chassisless SD Bus
	Highbridge				Lowbridge				Bus			Express		Coach				
	26'0" x 7'6"	26'0" x 8'0"	27'0" x 7'6"	27'0" x 8'0"	26'0" x 7'6"	26'0" x 8'0"	27'0" x 7'6"	27'0" x 8'0"	27'6" x 7'6"	30'0" x 7'6"	30'0" x 8'0"	27'6" x 7'6"	30'0" x 8'0"	27'6" x 7'6"	28'10" x 7'6"	30'0" x 7'6"	30'0" x 8'0"	
1946	52				154				368			6						
1947	150				302				265			64						
1948	196	16			526				266		50	8						
1949	136	16			369				283			21						16
1950	30		35	47	21		106	39	40	202	64	10		38			55	
1951			16	135		13	25	175	30	36	178	2	4				102	
1952		6		94	19	24	26	227	1							16	10	
1953				95				88										
1954	2	10		106				33			15							
1955	15		7	65	9					6								
1956				40														
1957			8	32											5		10	
1958																		
1959																		
1960																		
1961																		
1962																		
1963																		
1964																		
1965																		
Total	581	48	66	614	1400	37	157	562	1253	244	307	111	4	38	5	16	177	
	1309				2156				1804			115		236				16

Appendix 2

ECW production 1946-65 by programme year and body type

Prog Year	Prototype	Bristol Lodekka Double-deck								Bristol LS Single-deck			Single-deck on Other Underfloor Engined Chassis				
		LD	LLD	LDS	LDL	FS	FSF	FLF	FL	Bus	Exp	Coach	Ley'd Royal Tiger Bus	AEC Regal IV Coach	Ley'd RL Tr & Leop. Coach	Guy Arab UF Bus	SD on Guy Spl (GS) Bus
1946																	
1947																	
1948																	
1949	2																
1950										2							
1951													5	20	4		
1952										95	51	105		1			84
1953		176								230	14	123	5		5	1	
1954		167								156	25	83					
1955		329								81	43	18					
1956		377								139	43	38					
1957		417	6							73	18	49					
1958		243		9	1					1		5					
1959		308				40	1	1									
1960		85				137	62	67	25					5			
1961		77				79	92	155	8						5		
1962						128	52	287	12								
1963						185	11	232									
1964						125		123									
1965						102		351									
Total	2	2180	6	9	1	796	218	1216	45	777	194	421					
		4473								1392			10	26	14	1	84

Appendix 2
ECW production 1946-65 by programme year and body type

Prog Year	Bristol SC Single-deck		Single-deck Based on SC (Rehab)	Routemaster DD Coach	Bristol MW Single-deck			Bristol Rail Bus	Mobile Lab on Bedford 4x4	Bristol SU Single-deck			Bristol RE Single-deck		
	Stage	Coach			Bus	Exp	Coach			SUS Bus	SUL Bus	SUL Coach	RELL Bus	RELH Exp	RELH Coach
1946															
1947															
1948															
1949															
1950															
1951															
1952															
1953															
1954	2														
1955	72			1											
1956	57	7													
1957	42	13			111	28	2								
1958	9	10	32		118	25	102	2	1						
1959	46	10	4		127	44	55			16					
1960	39	10	6		132	20	45				29	8			
1961	9		6		126	24	81				18	9			
1962	1		6		185	29	82			3	6	21	1		1
1963					80	2	102			4	14		40	27	32
1964						10	36			2	11			24	37
1965					135	14					12		61		
Total	277	50			1014	206	505				90	38	102	91	70
	327		54	1	1725			2	1	25	128		223		

Appendix 3
Lodekka rear platform designs.

The rear-entrance Lodekka types had alternative platform designs which were identified by a design number, as follows:-

Lodekka LD and related types

No. 1 Open platform, thin construction, single-piece rectangular rear window with small-radius corners.

No. 2 Open or closed type, thicker platform, with two narrow rear windows having large-radius corners at top of centre pillar. Used mainly in the period up to 1956.

No. 3 Closed platform, thicker type, with two-leaf folding entrance doors, with two wider rear windows, but also having the large-radius corners at the top of the centre pillar. Emergency exit door hinged at nearside, taking in the nearside rear window. Widely used during the whole LD period.

No. 4 Similar to No. 3 but without doors, yet with provision to fit them later if required. Applied to a number of bodies for Crosville, as well as a few for Hants & Dorset, Lincolnshire, Southern National and Wilts & Dorset.

No. 5 Generally similar to No. 3 - exact differences not identified. This design is understood to have applied solely to three batches of LD for Western SMT (body numbers 9083-102, 1013242 and 10826-35.

No. 6 Open platform, similar to No. 1 but with thicker platform. Widely used from 1956.

No. 7 Similar to No. 3 but open platform without provision to fit doors. This design is understood to have applied to about 57 bodies supplied solely to Crosville.

FS and FL models

It is understood that only platform types No. 3 and No. 6 were used.

No. 3 This was basically similar to the corresponding closed platform design for the LD, but the two rear windows, still of the wider dimensions, had the larger corner radii at the outer top corners and the emergency door was hinged at the centre pillar.

No. 6 This open platform design was similar to the corresponding type used for the LD.

Platform design No. 2 used an unusual style of rear window, quite narrow yet divided even when no platform doors were provided, as here on Eastern National 1460 (563 CTW) an LD6B with body 7332 built in batch 154, seen in an official photograph dated 8th June 1955.

The No. 3 platform, as applied to FS-type buses, differed in having the emergency exit hinged on the centre pillar and the layout of the divided window was also changed, with the larger top corner radii at the outer edges, giving an effect perhaps more in keeping with the vehicle outline as a whole. Seen here is York-West Yorkshire 3820, originally YDX220 (NWU 264D) built in batch 403 and delivered in November 1966, though seen here in July 1980.

The No. 6 design was, in effect, No. 1 with a heavier-duty construction of the platform itself. This 'plain' rectangular rear window style was widely used on both LD and FS versions where doors were not required and is seen here on one of a batch of convertible open-top FS6G purchased by Bristol Omnibus for use at Weston-super-Mare, 8579 (869 NHT) with body 12289 being shown. It was built in batch 302 and delivered in November 1961.

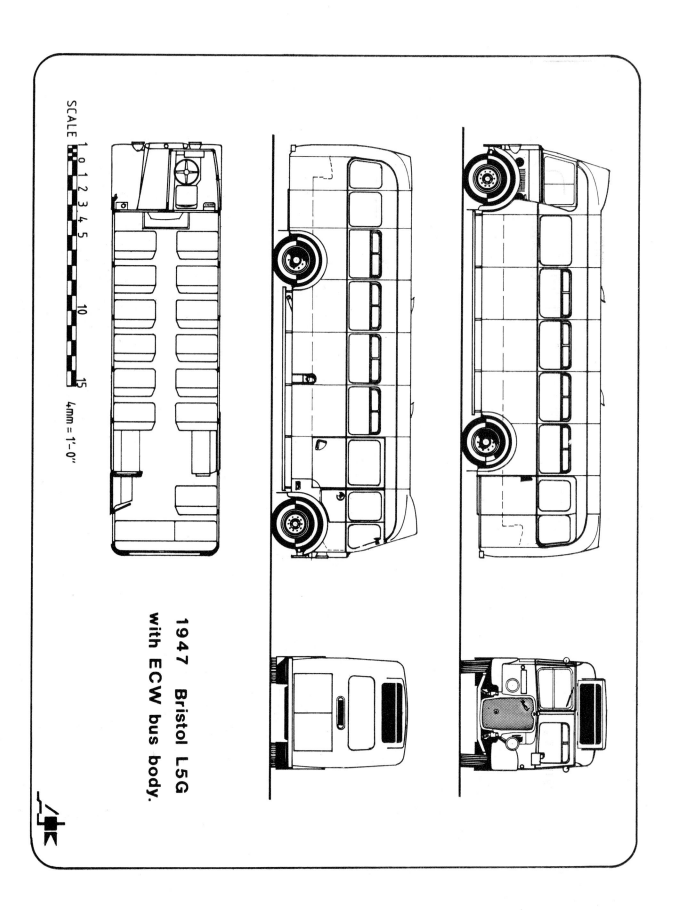

SCALE

0 1 2 3 4 5   10   15

4mm = 1'-0"

1947   Bristol L5G
with ECW bus body.

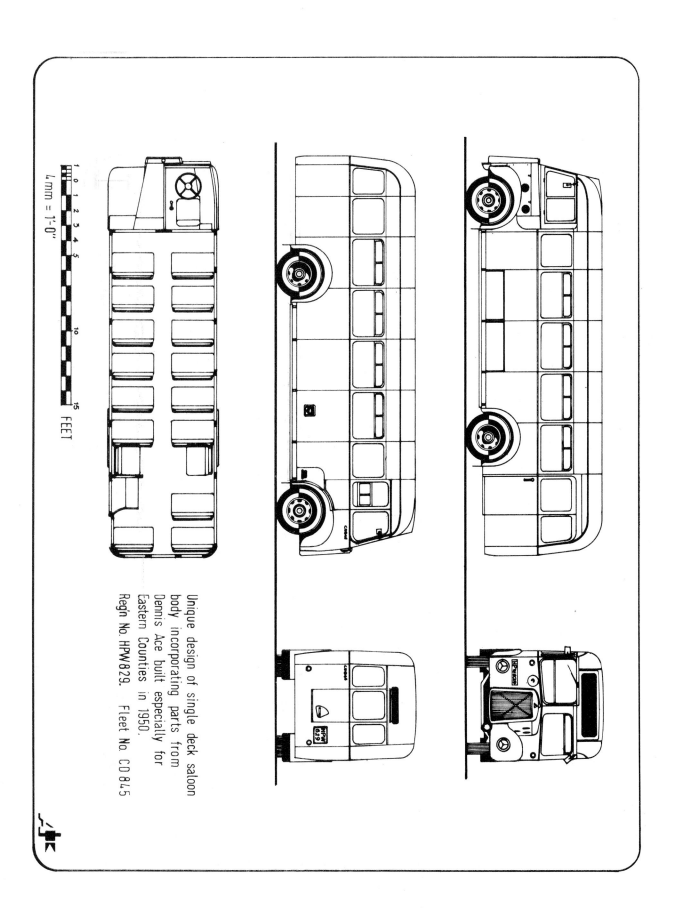

Unique design of single deck saloon body incorporating parts from Dennis Ace built especially for Eastern Counties in 1950. Regn No HPW829. Fleet No. CD 845

4 mm = 1'-0"

FEET

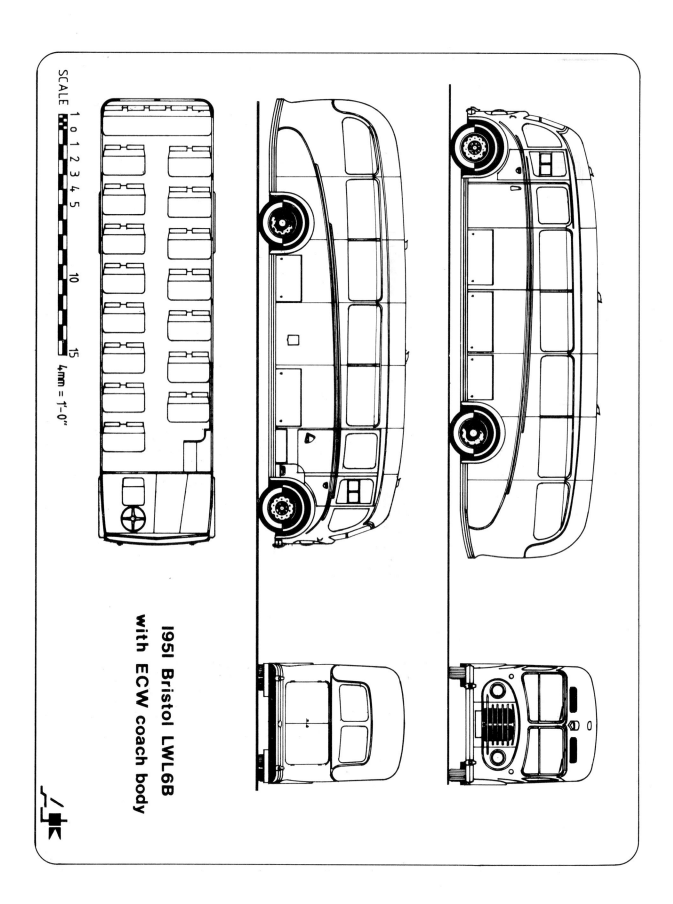

1951 Bristol LWL6B
with ECW coach body

SCALE

1 0 1 2 3 4 5   10   15

4mm = 1'-0"

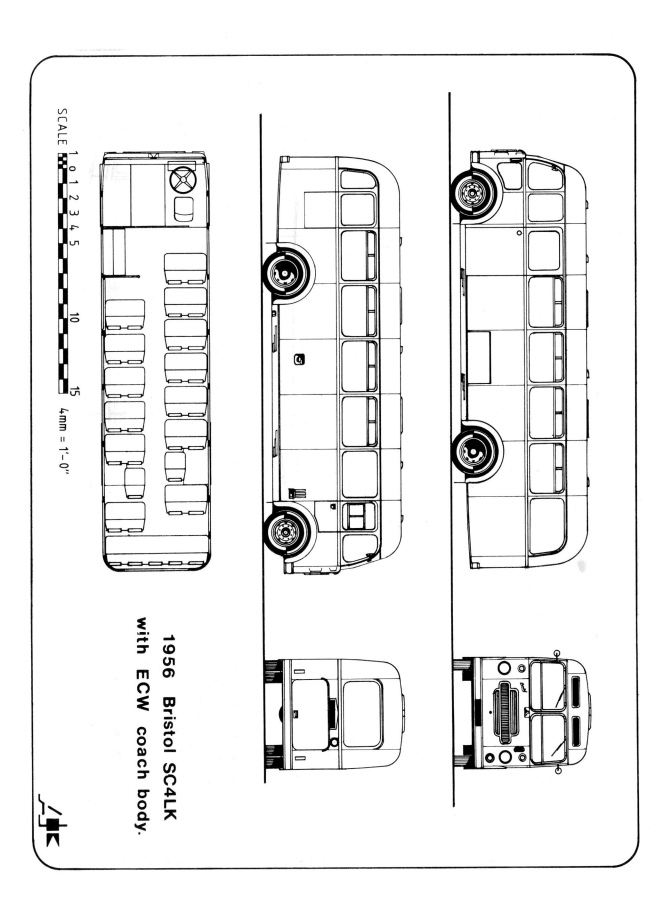

SCALE

0 1 2 3 4 5   10   15

4mm = 1'-0"

1956 Bristol SC4LK with ECW coach body.

Index

A full index to this volume and the next, covering the whole 1946-87 period, will appear at the end of the next volume.

Index to illustrations by operator